Question Bank for Agriculture

Question Bank for Agriculture

Ruchi Bajpai
B.Sc.(AG), M.Sc. (Seed Science & Technology)
Ph.D (Seed Science & Technology)
Associate Professor and Head of the Department
Department of Agriculture
Phonics Group of Institutions, Roorkee

Purna Jana
B.Sc. & M.Sc. (EVS), Ph.D (Forestry)
Assistant Professor
Department of Agriculture
Phonics Group of Institutions, Roorkee

Ram Vakil Rawat
B.Sc.(AG), M.Sc. (Entomolgy)
Assistant Professor
Department of Agriculture
Phonics Group of Institutions, Roorkee

A Paperback Division of

NEW INDIA PUBLISHING AGENCY

101, Vikas Surya Plaza, CU Block, LSC Market
Pitam Pura, New Delhi 110 034, India
Phone: + 91 (11)27 34 17 17 Fax: + 91(11) 27 34 16 16
Email: info@nipabooks.com
Web: www.nipabooks.com

Feedback at feedbacks@nipabooks.com

ISBN 978-93-86546-82-1

Composed, Designed & Printed in India

Preface

The prime objective of this book is to provide knowledge in the field of agriculture for both the graduate and post graduate students. This book is the collection of questions from several different subjects like Genetics, Seed science and technology, Biotechnology, Environmental Science, Entomology and Nematology. This book has been prepared keeping in view that course requirement in different competitive exams. Material content in the book largely comes from the notes prepared by the authors and some are memory based.

The topics mainly covered in this book are breeding programme, mode of reproduction, pollination, principles of pollinated crops, GMOs, seed production, seed testing, seed certification, seed storage, seed treatments, seed act, Mendel principles, dominance relationship, mutation, gene concept, inheritance, plant tissue culture, linkage, environmental pollution, biological diversity and its conservation, environmental problems and protection, sustainable development, natural resources, ecosystem, important species of plant parasitic nematodes, some important nematecides, history of entomology, morphology of insects, anatomy of insects, taxonomy of insects, some important harmful insects, important disease of field crops and horticultural crops.

I wish to acknowledge and express my sincere thanks to God and deep gratitude to the Phonics Group of Institutions, Roorkee especially the chairman **(Er. Cherub Jain)**, the director **(Dr. K.K. Gautam)&** **(Dr. M.S. Rana)** the assistant director (**Dr. Bhuvnender Chaudhary)** and the registrar **(Mr. Amit Gautam)** for their keen interest and providing us the opportunity to prepare the manuscript. I appreciate my colleagues **Mr. Ram V. Rawat, Dr. Purna Jana** for their immense help and support. Also I am thankful to **Ms. Garima Sharma, Mr. Nirbhay Ahlawat, Dr. R. A. Jan, Dr. Richa Chauhan, Ms Portia D. Singh and Ms. Prastuti Mishra** and staff **Mr. Ajay Kumar** of my department (Department of Agriculture) for their generous support. I also extend my thanks to one of our sincere student **Mr. Nitish Mandal** for his sincere hard work.

At the end I wish to record my deep sense of love and respect to my mom **Sadhana**, Dad **Dr. Ram bhushan**, brother **Anupam** & **Abhishek**, bhabhi **Jaya**, sister **Vandana**, jija **Jitendra**, niece & nephew **Anvi, Shubh, Krishna** and my husband **Anil** for their immense help and excellent moral support ever and always.

The effort and support of NIPA, New Delhi and his team as they worked really hard to give this book an attractive format.

Roorkee, 2017 **Ruchi Bajpai**

Contents

1

Genetics

Multiple Choice Based Questions and Answers

- The germplasm theory - Transmission of characters from one generation to other takes place only through germplasm. Any change in the germplasm will lead to change in the next generation - was proposed by

  i. Charles Darwin ii. **August Weismann**

  iii. Lamarck iv. Wolff

- The theory of Pangenesis was proposed by

  i. Tatum, E.L. ii. Johannsen, W.L.

  iii. **Charles Darwin** iv. Bridges, C.B.

- 'Mutation' the term was coined by

  i. Correns, Carl Erich ii. Morgan, T.H.

  iii. **Hugo, de Vries** iv. Tschemak, V.S.E.

- Who is called the 'Father of genetics'?

  i. Swammenrdam ii. Lamarck

  iii. Charles Darwin iv. **Mendel Gregor (Johann)**

- For normal growth and development of living organisms which cell division is required?

  i. Meiosis ii. **Mitosis**

  iii. Both iv. None of the above

- To maintain the purity which cell division is needed

  i. **Mitosis** ii. Meiosis

  iii. Both iv. None of the above

- In which cell division one member of homologous chromosomes moves to opposite pole during anaphase and generates variability due to segregation and recombination

  i. Mitosis ii. **Meiosis**

  iii. Both iv. None of the above

- The cell division helps in maintaining the chromosome number constant in a species is

  i. Mitosis ii. **Meiosis**

  iii. Both iv. None of the above

- Which cell division is essential for sexually reproducing species for the continuity of generation?

  i. **Meiosis** ii. Mitosis

  iii. Both iv. None of the above

- During diplotene stage in oocyte nuclei of both vertebrates and invertebrates and spermatocyte nuclei of Drosophila which chromosomes are found?

  i. Polytene ii. **Lampbrush**

  iii. Both iv. None of the above

- Balbiani (1881) reported the chromosome in salivary glands of dipteran insects is

  i. Lampbrush ii. **Polytene**

  iii. Both iv. None of the above

- Balbiani ring is found in

  i. Lampbrush chromosome ii. **Polytene chromosome**

  iii. Both iv. None of the above

- Some species possess extra chromosome which are not members of normal chromosome complements are called

  i. A chromosome ii. **B chromosome**

  iii. Both iv. None of the above

- Longley, 1927 and Randolph, 1928 were first reported B chromosome in

  i. **Maize** ii. Rice

  iii. Drosophila iv. None of the above

- The meiotic behaviour of B chromosomes is studied during

  i. Zygotene stage ii. Deplotene stage

  iii. **Pachytene stage** iv. Leptotene stage

- Darkly staining region of chromosomes during interphase, usually inactive in transcription, found near centromere and telomere is

  i. Euchromatin ii. **Heterochromatin**

  iii. Both iv. None of the above

- Loss of a segment from a chromosome is called

  i. Tandem ii. **Deletion**

  iii. Duplication iv. Translocation

- Duplication with normal sequence (similar to original segment) of genes is called

  i. **Tandem** ii. Deletion

  iii. Duplication iv. Translocation

- One way or reciprocal exchange of segments between non-homologous chromosomes is called

  i. Tandem ii. Deletion

  iii. Duplication iv. **Translocation**

- At anaphase movement of two normal chromosomes towards one pole and that of two translocated chromosomes to another pole is called

  i. Tandem ii. Reverse displaced

  iii. **Alternate segregation** iv. Translocation

- Inversion in which centromere is not involved is called

  i. Pericentric inversion ii. **Paracentric inversion**

  iii. Both iv. None of the above

- A polyploidy organism which originates by combining complete chromosomes sets from two or more species is known as

  i. **Allopolyploid** ii. Autopolyploid

  iii. Aneuploid iv. Autotetraploid

- Raphanobrassica is example of artificially synthesized alloploid between

  i. *Raphanus oleracea* and *Brassica sativus*

  ii. ***Raphanus sativus* and *Brassica oleracea***

  iii. *Raphanus glutinosa* and *Brassica sativus*

  iv. None of the above

- The change in chromosome number which involves one or few chromosomes of the genome is called

  i. Allopolyploidy ii. Autopolyploidy

  iii. **Aneuploidy** iv. Autotetraploidy

- A condition which refers to interaction of two or more genes, thus involves two or more loci is called

  i. **Epistasis** ii. Dominance

  iii. Both iv. None

- A situation where recessive gene can express only in hemizygous condition is called

  i. Epistasis ii. **Dominance**

  iii. Both iv. None

- The linkage between two or more either dominant (AB) or recessive (ab) alleles is referred to as

  i. Repulsion ii. **Coupling**

  iii. Both iv. None

- The linkage of genes which are located in sex chromosomes are called

  i. Incomplete linkage ii. Autosomal linkage

  iii. **X-chromosomal linkage** iv. None

- Three point test cross, helps in mapping of chromosome, provides which of following useful information

  i. About the sequence of genes

  ii. About the recombination frequencies between genes

  iii. **Both**

  iv. None

- The character located on sex chromosomes or autosomes and express in one sex only is called

  i. Sex-linked character ii. **Sex-limited character**

  iii. Sex-influenced character iv. None

- The character includes characters not related to sex is called

  i. **Sex-linked character** ii. Sex-limited character

  iii. Sex-influenced character iv. None

- Colour blindness in man is a

  i. **Sex-linked character** ii. Sex-limited character

  iii. Sex-influenced character iv. None

- The syndrome which possess the characteristics of an abnormal human male who has XXY chromosome constitution is called

  i. Turner's syndrome ii. **Klinefelter's syndrome**

  iii. Both iv. None

- Model which explains the accurate replication of DNA

  i. Dispersive replication ii. Conservative replication

  iii. Semiconservative replication iv. **All of the above**

- Important experiment which supports that DNA replication is semi-conservative
  - i. Meselson and Stahl experiment
  - ii. Cairns experiment
  - iii. Taylor's experiment
  - iv. **All of the above**

- Components of RNA are
  - i. Nitrogenous base, Ribose sugar
  - ii. Ribose Sugar, Phosphate group
  - iii. Nitrogenous base, Phosphate group
  - iv. **Nitrogenous base, Ribose sugar and Phosphate group**

- The RNA which constitutes about 80% of the total cellular RNA is
  - i. **R-RNA**
  - ii. M-RNA
  - iii. T-RNA
  - iv. M-RNA and T-RNA

- Synthesis of DNA from RNA molecule is called
  - i. **Reverse transcription**
  - ii. Transcription
  - iii. Both
  - iv. None of the above

- The mechanism of transcription consists
  - i. Initiation and Termination
  - ii. Elongation and Termination
  - iii. **Initiation, Elongation and Termination**
  - iv. None of the above

- TFIID consists of
  - i. TBP
  - ii. TAFs
  - iii. **Both**
  - iv. None of the above

- In some eukaryotic cells an enzyme is found with reverse transcription activity is called

  i. Telomerase　　ii. Reverse Transcriptase

  iii. **Both**　　iv. None of the above

- In the process of Translation start codon is

  i. **AUG**　　ii. UAG

  iii. UGA　　iv. None of the above

- In the process of Translation stop codon is

  i. AUG　　ii. GUA

  iii. **UGA**　　iv. GAU

- In the operon model of gene regulation type of gene involved

  i. Structural gene　　ii. Operator gene

  iii. Regulator gene　　iv. **All of the above**

- Structural genes of lac operon are

  i. lac Z, lac Y and lac V　　ii. lac Y, lac A and lac B

  iii. lac A, lac Z and lac C　　iv. **lac Z, lac Y and lac A**

- Types of operon model

  i. Inducible operon　　ii. Repressible operon

  iii. **Both**　　iv. None of the above

- The process of inhibition of transcription is called

  i. **Repression**　　ii. Induction

  iii. Both　　iv. None of the above

- The term genetics was proposed by

  i. **William Bateson (1902)**　　ii. N. Grew (1682)

  iii. Camerarious (1694)　　iv. Thomas Fairchild (1717)

- The theory which states that crossing over takes place due to breakage and reunion of non-sister chromatids is

  i. **Breakage and reunion theory**

  ii. Copy choice theory

  iii. Classical theory

  iv. None of the above

- Gene transfer can be achieved by

  i. Via plasmid and through direct uptake

  ii. Particle bombardment and micro injection

  iii. By micro injection and through direct uptake

  iv. **By all of the above**

- In genetics chi-square test is applied for the purpose

  i. To test the validity of various segregation ratio

  ii. For detection of linkage

  iii. In study of gene frequencies in population genetics.

  iv. **All of the above**

- Chi-square cannot properly be applied to distributions in which the frequency of any class is less than

  i. **5** ii. 6

  iii. 7 iv. 10

- Statistical procedure which are used for the polygenic trait analysis are

  i. Arithmetic mean, Measures of dispersion, Analysis of variance

  ii. Analysis of variance, Analysis of co-variance, Tests of significance

  iii. Correlation analysis, Regression analysis, Tests of significance

  iv. **All of above**

- Basic principles of experimental design are

  i. Replication and randomization

  ii. Randomization and local control

  iii. Replication and error control

  iv. **Replication, randomization and local controlm**

- The design which is used when the experimental material is limited and homogeneous is known as

  i. **Completely randomized design**

  ii. Randomized block design

  iii. Latin square design

  iv. Split plot design

- The principle of local control is not adopted in case of

  i. **Completely randomized design**

  ii. Randomized block design

  iii. Latin square design

  iv. Split plot design

- The design which provides highly précised result because the fertility variation is controlled in two directions which reduces the standard error is

  i. Completely randomized design

  ii. Randomized block design

  iii. **Latin square design**

  iv. Split plot design

- The design suitable for pot culture and when the experimental material is limited and homogeneous is

  i. **Completely randomized design**

  ii. Randomized block design

  iii. Latin square design

  iv. Split plot design

- Basic requirements for tissue culture technique are

  i. Aseptic condition, Control of temperature

  ii. Proper culture media and Sub culturing

  iii. Aseptic condition and Proper culture media

  iv. **All of the above**

- The main problem in micropopagation technique is

  i. Somaclonal variation

  ii. Variation in chromosome number due to continuous sub-culturing

  iii. **Both**

  iv. None of the above

- The trait governed by non-additive genes is

  i. **Oligogenic traits** ii. Polygenic traits

  iii. Both iv. None of the above

- Of the followings which is/are the cytoplasmic inheritance

  i. Maternal effects

  ii. Inheritence due to ineffective particles

  iii. Cytoplasmic inheritance

  iv. **All of above**

- Synthesis occurs only during interphase in

  i. Cytoplasmic DNA ii. **Nuclear DNA**

  iii. Both iv. None of above

- Type of cytoplasmic inheritance is/are

  i. Plasmid inheritance ii. Mitochondrial inheritance

  iii. **Both** iv. None of the above

- The syndrome refers to the characteristics of an abnormal female who has an XO chromosome constitution is

  i. **Turner's syndrome** ii. Klinefelter's syndrome

  iii. Down syndrome iv. None of the above

- The syndrome refers to the characteristics of an abnormal human male who has an XXY chromosome constitution is

  i. Turner's syndrome ii. **Klinefelter's syndrome**

  iii. Down syndrome iv. None of the above

- Allosomes are

  i. Generally control traits other than sex

  ii. **Usually determine sex of an individual**

  iii. Both

  iv. None of above

- The theory according which first crossing over occurs and then chiasma is formed is

  i. Classical theory ii. **Chiasma type theory**

  iii. Copy choice theory iv. None of the above

- The theory which states that the entire recombinant section or part arises from the newly synthesized section is

  i. Breakage and reunion theory ii. **Copy choice theory**

  iii. Classical theory iv. None of the above

- The linkage of dominant allele with that of the recessive allele (Ab or aB) is known as

  i. Coupling ii. **Repulsion**

  iii. Both iv. None of the above

❒ The phenomenon where a gene having more than one phenotypic effect is called

i. Pleiotropism ii. Pleiotropy

iii. **Both** iv. None of the above

❒ The gene interaction where two dominant alleles have similar effect when they are separate, but produce enhanced effect when they come together is called

i. **Polymeric gene interaction** ii. Pleiotropic gene interaction

iii. Both iv. None

❒ When a dominant allele at either of two loci can mask the expression of recessive alleles at the two loci, it is known as

i. Dominant epistasis ii. **Duplicate dominant epistasis**

iii. Recessive epistasis iv. None of above

❒ When a dominant allele at one locus can mask the expression of both alleles at another locus, it is known as

i. **Dominant epistasis** ii. Recessive epistasis

iii. Duplicate epistasis iv. None of the above

❒ A cross between two genotypes in which the order of male and female is reversed is called

i. **Reciprocal cross** ii. Back cross

iii. Direct cross iv. Test cross

❒ Both alleles express their phenotypes in heterozygote is

i. **Codominance** ii. Incomplete dominance

iii. Dominance iv. None

❒ Polyhaploids which develop from an auto polyploidy species is

i. **Autohaploid** ii. Aneuhaploid

iii. Dihaploid iv. None

- Any change in chromosome number from the diploid state is called

  i. **Heteroploidy** ii. Euploidy

  iii. Homoploidy iv. None of above

- The change in entire genome is called

  i. Heteroploidy ii. **Euploidy**

  iii. Homoploidy iv. None of above

- Colchicine is used in induction of

  i. **Polyploidy** ii. Haploidy

  iii. Both iv. None

- Inversion was first discovered by Sturtevant in 1926 in

  i. **Drosophila** ii. Maize

  iii. Nicotina iv. Mouse

- Translocation is

  i. **When one way or reciprocal transfer of segments between non-homologous chromosomes occurs.**

  ii. When there is mutual exchange of segments between non-homologous chromosomes occurs

  iii. Both

  iv. None

- Reciprocal translocation is

  i. When one way or reciprocal transfer of segments between non-homologous chromosomes occurs

  ii. **When there is mutual exchange of segments between non-homologous chromosomes occurs**

  iii. Both

  iv. None

- The pollen fertility is reduced in the presence of

  i. **Deletion** ii. Detection

  iii. Duplication iv. Interstitial deletion

- Structural changes usually takes place during

  i. **Interphase** ii. Metaphase

  iii. Anaphase iii. Telophase

- Chromosomes which do not differ in morphology and number in male and female sex and rarely contain sex determining genes are

  i. Allosomes ii. **Autosomes**

  iii. Dicentric chromosome iv. None

- Normal member of chromosome complements of a species which are essential for normal growth and development is

  i. **A-chromosome** ii. B-chromosome

  iii. C-chromosome iv. D-chromosome

- A chromosome in which centromere is located very near to one end or has sub-terminal position is called

  i. Holokinetic chromosome ii. **Acrocentric chromosome**

  iii. Acentric choromosome iv. Metacentric chromosome

- Diffused position of centromere can be found in

  i. **Holokinetic chromosome** ii. Telocentric chromosome

  iii. Acrocentric chromosome iv. Meta centric chromosome

- Terminal position of centromere can be found in

  i. Holokinetic chromosome ii. **Telocentric chromosome**

  iii. Acrocentric chromosome iv. Meta centric chromosome

- Basic number is

  i. The somatic chromosome number of a species

  ii. **The gametic chromosome number of a true diploid species**

  iii. The half of the somatic chromosome number of a species

  iv. None

- For the continuity of generation which cell division is essential?

  i. Mitosis ii. **Meiosis**

  iii. None iv. All

- Which cell division confirms growth of vegetative parts?

  i. **Mitosis** ii. Meiosis

  iii. None iv. All

- Of the followings the plastid type is/are

  i. Leucoplast ii. Chromoplast

  iii. Chloroplast iv. **All**

- Coupling and repulsion concepts of linkage has been discovered by Batesonand Punnett (1905) on

  i. Drosophila ii. **Garden pea**

  iii. Maize iv. Wheat

- Artificial copy of yeast gene was prepared by

  i. Barbara McClintock ii. **Har Gobind Khurana**

  iii. Mendel iv. Jacob

- How the genetic components of the cell nucleus control the synthesis of protein was discovered by

  i. **Har Gobind Khurana** ii. Jacob

  iii. Watson and Crick iv. None of above

- The control of hereditary disease especially inborn error of metabolism is dealt by

  i. Cytogenetics ii. **Euphenics**

  iii. Eugenics iv. Mendelian genetics

- A combination of deoxyribose sugar and nitrogenous base is called

  i. Nucleotide ii. **Nucleoside**

  iii. Both iv. None

- Components of DNA are

  i. Nirtrogenous base and nucleoside

  ii. **Nucleoside and phosphate group**

  iii. Nirtrogenous base and phosphate group

  iv. Deoxyribose sugar and nitrogenous base

- The theory "Only those organs of the body developed well which were in great use over long period of time and those organs which were in less or no use became reduced and finally disappeared" was formulated by

  i. Linnaeus ii. **Lamarck**

  iii. Darwin iv. Mendel

- The condition "Iojap" is found in

  i. **Maize** ii. Rice

  iii. Sugercane iv. Mustard

- Theory of germplasm stated

  i. The body of an organism contains two types of cells; somatic cells having somatoplasm and reproductive cells or germ cells with germplasm

  ii. The somatoplasm cannot form germplasm but germplasm is meant for reproduction and can form somatoplasm as well

  iii. Changes in the structure of somatoplasm caused by environment cannot influence the reproductive cells or germplasm whereas the changes occurring in germplasm influence the progeny

  iv. **All of the above**

- Chromosome theory of heredity was stated by

  i. **Thomas Hunt Morgan (1910)**

  ii. Thomas Hunt Morgan (1901)

  iii. Galton (1900)

  iv. None of the above

- "The gene is a factor for determining one or more hereditary characters in all organisms" was stated by

  i. **T.H. Morgan (1910)** ii. Nurenberg (1901)

  iii. Galton (1900) iv. None of the above

- For the discovery of induction of mutation by x-ray in 1946 the Nobel prize was received by

  i. T.H. Morgan ii. **H.J.Muller**

  iii. A. Kornberg and Ochoa iv. Holley

- The discovery of double helix model of DNA was done by

  i. **Watson, Crick and Wilkins** ii. H.J.Muller

  iii. A. Kornberg and Ochoa iv. Holley

- Discovery of regulator genes and operator genes which regulate the activity of structural genes was done by

  i. T.H. Morgan ii. **Jacob, Monad and Leowulf**

  iii. H.J.Muller iv. Holley

- For the outstanding work on genetic code Nobel prize was received in 1968 by

  i. Nurenberg ii. Hargovind Khorana

  iii. Holley iv. **All of the above**

- Back cross is

  i. **When heterozygous individuals of F_1 generation are crossed with one of the parental type (P) individuals**

  ii. When the F_1 hybrid individuals are crossed with dominant homozygous parent

  iii. When F_1 hybrid individuals are crossed with homozygous recessive parent

  iv. None of the above

- Out cross is

  i. **When the F_1 hybrid individuals are crossed with dominant homozygous parent**

  ii. When heterozygous individuals of F_1 generation are crossed with one of the parental type (P) individuals

  iii. When F_1 hybrid individuals are crossed with homozygous recessive parent

  iv. None of the above

- Test cross is

  i. **When F_1 hybrid individuals are crossed with homozygous recessive parent**

  ii. When the F_1 hybrid individuals are crossed with dominant homozygous parent

  iii. When heterozygous individuals of F_1 generation are crossed with one of the parental type (P) individuals

  iv. None of the above

- From the result of dihybrid experiment Mendel concluded

  i. The members of two sets of allele segregated in F_2 generation

  ii. The allele of one set behaved independently with respect to those of the other set at the time of combination

  iii. **Both**

  iv. None of the above

- Which of the following is easier, quicker device used to illustrate possible combinations resulting from the crosses

  i. Punnett square
  ii. **Forked line**
  iii. Checker board
  iv. None of the above

- Sutton and Boveri in 1904 followed the points of Wilhelm Roux and formulated a theory called

  i. **The chromosome theory of heredity**
  ii. The theory of segregation
  iii. The theory of independent assortment
  iv. None of the above

- Mendel in his two laws of heredity stated that the characters of the organisms were determined by "factors". Factors are actually

  i. **Genes**
  ii. Chromosome
  iii. Allele
  iv. None of the above

- The "factor" stated by Mendel later termed as genes by

  i. **W. Johannsen**
  ii. Leowulf
  iii. H.J.Muller
  iv. Holley

- Multiple allelism was discovered by

  i. **L. Cuenot**
  ii. Bateson
  iii. Johannsen
  iv. Mendel

- The phenomenon of incomplete dominance was described by

  i. **Kolreuter**
  ii. Bateson
  iii. Johannsen
  iv. Cuenot

- Black feathered fowl is crossed with white feathered hen, the F_1 individuals are blue feathered. It is an example of

  i. **Incomplete dominance**
  ii. Complete dominance
  iii. Over dominance
  iv. Co-dominance

- The type of dominance where phenotype of heterozygote is more extreme than that of either parent is

  i. Incomplete dominance ii. Complete dominance
  iii. **Over dominance** iv. Co-dominance

- The type of dominance where heterozygous shows the phenotype of both homozygotes or parents rather than expressing an intermediate phenotype is

  i. Incomplete dominance ii. Complete dominance
  iii. Over dominance iv. **Co-dominance**

- AB blood group in man is an example of parent is

  i. Incomplete dominance ii. Complete dominance
  iii. **Co-dominance** iv. Over dominance

- Genes those are influenced by other genes or the environment and are generally governed by one or more genes with large easily detectable effects are

  i. **Oligogenes** ii. Modifying genes
  iii. Polygenes iv. None of the above

- The traits determined by oligogenes show distinct classes are known as

  i. **Qualitative characters** ii. Quantitative characters
  iii. Both iv. None of the above

- Genes those are influenced by the genetic background and by the environment are generally governed by specific genes are called

  i. Oligogenes ii. Modifying genes
  iii. **Polygenes** iv. None of the above

- Polygene affected characters are called

  i. Qualitative characters ii. **Quantitative characters**
  iii. Both iv. None of the above

- Genes those have little or no effect of their own but increase or decrease the expression of other major genes are called

  i. Oligogenes ii. **Modifying genes**
  iii. Poly genes iv. None of the above

- The ability of a gene to express itself in an individual that carries it is called

  i. **Penetrance** ii. Incomplete penetrance
  iii. Expressivity iv. Threshold character

- An organism may be of a genotype aa or A^- but may not express the phenotype associated with its genotype due to modifying effect of the environment or due to modifiers – such genes are supposed to have

  i. Penetrance ii. **Incomplete penetrance**
  iii. Complete penetrance iv. Expressivity

- The gene which expresses itself in every individual that carries it is said to have

  i. Penetrance ii. Incomplete penetrance
  iii. **Complete penetrance** iv. Expressivity

- The extent to which a given genotype is expressed phenotypically in an individual is

  i. Penetrance ii. Incomplete penetrance
  iii. Complete penetrance iv. **Expressivity**

- The characters whose development depends upon a specific environment are referred to as

  i. Penetrance ii. **Threshold character**
  iii. Expressivity iv. None of the above

- The net effect on the trait depends upon the combined action of several genes, each of which has a small effect on the same trait. Such genes are called

  i. Cumulative genes ii. Poly genes
  iii. **Both** iv. None of the above

- During gamete formation the cell containing both dominant and both recessive genes underwent mitotic reproduction to a greater extent than the others thereby giving specific ratio is called

  i. **Reduplication hypothesis** ii. Duplication hypothesis

  iii. Both iv. None of the above

- In higher plants and animals, macrogametes contain large amount of cytoplasm but microgametes have essentially negligible amount of cytoplasm, therefore, under such condition most of cytoplasmic factors are transmitted to the offsprings through the ovary of mother- this is known as

  i. Maternal inheritance ii. Trans-ovarian transmission

  iii. **Both** iv. None of the above

- The tendency of genes to be inherited in groups is called

  i. **Linkage** ii. Repulsion

  iii. Both iv. None

- The original parental gene arrangement on the homologous chromosomes is called parental combination and the new gene combinations arising out of crossing over are called

  i. Cross over types ii. Exchange products

  iii. Recombinants iv. **All of above**

- The hypothesis represents the best explanation to date to account for the formation of recombinants is

  i. **Darlington's theory of crossing over**

  ii. Uhl's theory

  iii. Belling's copy choice theory

  iv. Janssen's classical theory

- Most of the cytoplasmically inherited characters would follow the maternal (mother) lines i.e. called

  i. **Uniparental mode of transmission**

  ii. Maternal inheritance

  iii. Transovarian transmission

  iv. None of the above

2

Seed Technology

Multiple Choice Based Questions and Answers

- The plant tissue or organs excised and used for invitro culture is known as

  A. Transgenic plants B. Bulb

  C. Callus D. **Ex plant**

- In hybrid seed production male sterile line crossed with which one of the following line

  A. **R line** B. A line

  C. C line D. Inbread line

- Over dominance hypothesis was given by

  A. East B. Darwin

  C. **East and Shull** D. Jones

- Removal of all type plants from field is known as

  A. **Roguing** B. Purity test

  C. Mechanical admixture D. Mutation

- Progeny of the breeder seed is

  A. Nucleus seed B. T L seed

  C. **Foundation seed** D. Certified seed

- The tag color of Breeder seed class of seed

  A. Blue B. **Golden yellow**

  C. White D. Azure blue

- Tag size of Breeder seed (L X B)

  A. **12** X **6 Cm** B. 15 X 7.5 Cm

  C. 15 X 10 Cm D. 10 X 5 Cm

- The tag color of Foundation seed

  A. Azure Blue B. **White**

  C. Opel Green D. Sky Blue

- Tag size of Foundation and Certified class of seeds

  A. 15 X 10 Cm B. **15** X **7.5 Cm**

  C. 15 X 7 Cm D. 12 X 6 Cm

- Tag color of Certified class of seeds

  A. White B. Opel Green

  C. **Azuer Blue** D. Golden yellow

- Tag color of Truthful Label seeds

  A. **Opel Green** B. Azure Blue

  C. White D. Green

- Tag size of TL seeds (L X B)

  A. 15 X 7.5 Cm B. **15** X **10 Cm**

  C. 12 X 6 Cm D. 15 X 7.1 Cm

- The progency of Foundation seeds

  A. Nucleus seed B. **Certified seeds**

  C. Breeder seed D. TL seeds

- In India how many generations system followed for seed production

  A. 2 B. 4

  C. **3** D. 5

- The effect of foreign pollen on the endosperm is known as

  A. Xenia B. **Metaxenia**

  C. Mutation D. Crossing

- Seed moisture content for one year storage

  A. 11 to 13% B. **10 to 12 %**

  C. 15 to13% D. 18 to 15%

- As per the Harrington rule addition of relative humidity and temperature should be

  A. 50 B. 70

  C. 110 D. **100**

- The body within the ovary of the flower that becomes the seed after fertilzation is called as

  A. **Ovule** B. Spike

  C. Glume D. Rakeme

- The study of pollen is termed as

  A. Cartilinology B. Palentology

  C. Ornithology D. **Paelonology**

- Seedlessness in fruits or formation of fruit without fertilization is called as

  A. Perfect Fertilization B. Parthenogenesis

  C. Endocarpy D. **Parthenocarpy**

- The moisture content for the safe storage of cereals is

  A. 1 - 2 % B. **12 - 14 %**

  C. 18 - 20 % D. 25 - 28 %

- Central Tobbacco Research Institute was situated at

  A. Hybrid derivative B. **Rajamundry**

  C. Ideotype D. Cybrid line

- Directorate of Maize Research was situated at

  A. Rajendranagar B. **New Delhi**

  C. Barackpore D. Cuttack

- The reduction or loss in vigour and fertility as a result of Inbreeding is called as

  A. **Inbreeding depression** B. Heritability

  C. Co-heritability D. Heterosis

- International Rice Research Institute is situated at

  A. Rome B. Lime

  C. El Batan D. **Manila**

- The gradual loss of variability in the cultivated forms and in their wild relatives is reffered to as

  A. Genetic dhift B. Genetic shift

  C. **Genetic erosion** D. None of the above

- In crops, grow out test is done for the varification of its trueness to type or variety, which is termed as

  A. **Genetic purity** B. Crop purity

  C. Dockage purity D. Seed purity

- The minimum number of counts to be taken for an area upto two hectares in Wheat during field isnpection are

  A. 15 B. 10

  C. 3 D. **5**

- The outer bract of the flowers of grasses sometimes refferred to as flowering glume is called as

  A. **Lemma** B. Glume

  C. Palea D. Anther

- Tz test colour of living tissues of seed change to

  A. Yellow B. Green

  C. **Red** D. Blue

- Effect of pollen grains on the material tissues e.g. on the fruit quality in date palm or the effect of foreign pollen on the endosperm colouration is called as

  A. Paramutation B. **Metaxenia**

  C. Penetrance D. Regulon

- The crop in which the cooling germination test was normally used

  A. Cotton B. Wheat

  C. Amaranthes D. **Soybean**

- A group of similar plants in structural features and performance is known as

  A. Clone B. Inbred line

  C. **Variety** D. Pure line

- The heterosis estimated over the superior parent is known as

  A. **Heterobeltiosis** B. Clonal degeneration

  C. Standard heterosis D. Inbreeding depression

- National Bureau of Plant Genetic Resources is situated at

  A. Chennai B. Mumbai

  C. **New Delhi** D. Calcutta

- The superiority of an F_1 hybrid over both its parents in terms of yield and some other characters is defined as

  A. Inbreeding depression B. **Heterosis**

  C. Clonal regeneration D. Heterobeltiosis

- The fruit derived from one carpel and splitting along one side is called as

  A. Spike B. Achene

  C. Caryopsis D. **Follicle**

- The progency of the breeder seeds and the source of registered and certified seed is called

  A. Breeder seed B. Certified seed

  C. Basic seed D. **Foundation seed**

- The blotter method of seed health testing detects primarily the disease organisms like

  A. **Fungi** B. Virus

  C. Bacteria D. Nematodes

- The pollen from a flower of one plant falls on the stigmas of other flowers of the same plant is known as

  A. **Geitanogamy** B. Gametogenesis

  C. Sporogenesis D. Cytogenesis

- The sum total of all the genes present in a random mating population at a given time is called as

  A. Germplasm B. **Gene pool**

  C. Gene drift D. Gene flow

- Emergence of normal seedlings from the seeds under ideal conditions of light, temperature, moisture, oxygen and nutrients is called

  A. Fertilization B. Detasseling

  C. Pollination D. **Germination**

- The chemical by which seedless grapes can be produceed is called

  A. **Gibberellins** B. Ethanol

  C. Auxins D. Catalyses

- ICPH-8, pigeon pea hybrid is released in the year

  A. **1991** B. 1970

  C. 2000 D. 1996

- Thename of the chemical, which on spraying will enhance complete panical exertion in hybrid seed production of rice is

  A. Glutamic acid B. Ethanol

  C. Lactic acid D. **Gibberellic acid**

- Cotton hybrid was first released in the year

  A. 1991 B. **1970**

  C. 2000 D. 1996

- The point where the integuments meet at the nucellar apex has been known as

  A. Radicle B. Hypocotyle

  C. Hilium D. **Microphyle**

- The Grow Out Test in crops is done for verification

  A. Physical purity B. **Genetic Purity**

  C. Germination D. Dockage Purity

- The presence of stamens and pistils in different flowers on the same plant is called as

  A. Diocious B. Dihybrid

  C. Monohybrid D. **Monoecious**

- The original seed of a variety available with the producing breeder or any other recognized breeder of the crop is called

  A. Breeder seed B. Certified seed

  C. **Nucleus seed** D. Foundation seed

❐ Loos smut is an

A. **Internally seed borne** B. Externally seed borne

C. Air borne D. Insect borne

❐ Percent oil content is highest in the moisture content for the safe storage of cereals is

A. Sesamum B. GroundnutC.

Castor D. Soyabean

❐ The seeds, which can be dried to low moisture content and stored at low temperatures without loosing their viability are called as

A. Naked seed B. **Orthodox seed**

C. Synthetic seed D. Basic seed

❐ Separartion of the field of a variety from that of another variety of the same crop to prescribed standard distance to avoid contamination is called

A. Distance separation B. **Isolation**

C. Hybridization D. Introgression

❐ The technique in which early formed ear heads of the first tiller are pulled so as to enhance the flowering of all the tillers in bajra is called as

A. Emasculation B. Detasseling

C. Desilking D. **Jerking**

❐ The standard for germination % (min) for certified seed of gram is

A. **85** B. 75

C. 80 D. 90

❐ The phase after imbibition and before radicle protrusion during germination is called as

A. Interphase B. **Lag phase**

C. Prophase D. Log phase

- National Dairy Research Institute is situated at

  A. **Karnal** B. Ludhiana

  C. New Delhi D. Chandigarh

- Plants in which the cotyledons appear below the surface of the soil is called as

  A. Hypergeal B. **Hypogeal**

  C. Endogeal D. Epigeal

- The major 'auxin' in developing seed is

  A. **IAA** B. ABA

  C. BOAA D. BOE

- Central Rice Research Institute was situated at

  A. Barrackpore B. Rajmundry

  C. **Cuttack** D. Rajendranagar

- The first hybrid in pigeon pea in the world is

  A. ICPH 12 B. PH 102

  C. IIPH 4 D. **ICPH-8**

- Occurrence of pollination and fertilization in an unopened flower bud i.e, flower do not open at all and 100 % self – fertilization will occur is called

  A. Chasmogamy B. Cheiropterophilly

  C. Anemophily D. **Cliestogamy**

- How many primary samples will be taken from three containers of 100 kg ?

  A. 5 B. 3

  C. 15 D. **9**

- Difference between seed and grain is

  A. Cost B. Seed quality

  C. **Genetic purity** D. Seed processing

- The male sterility that is dependent upon the action of genes carried in the nucleus with the particular cytoplasm is called as

  A. Genetic male sterility

  B. **Cytoplasmic -genetic male sterility**

  C. Cytoplasmic male sterility

  D. Self incompatibility

- Removal of water vapour from the air in storage of food grains

  A. Aeration B. Processing

  C. **Dehumidification** D. Heating

- Removal of male flower from the female parent in maize is commonly known as

  A. Emasculation B. Pollination

  C. **Detasseling** D. Tasseling

- The male sterility system that is used in hybrid seed production of rice is known as

  A. Genetic male sterility

  B. Cytoplasmic male sterility

  C. **Cytoplasmic - genetic male sterility**

  D. Selfincompability

- Fanning mill is

  A. **Air screen cleaner** B. Hammer mill

  C. Rice mill D. Blower

- Maturation of male and female reproductive organ of a hermaphrodite flower at different times is called as

  A. **Dichogamy** B. Plasmogamy

  C. Cliestogamy D. Herchogamy

- The presence of stamens and pistils in different plant is called as

  A. **Dioecious** B. Dihybrid

  C. Monohybrid D. Monoecism

- The growing point of the embryo which give rise to the shoot, or the above ground part of the plant can be termed as

  A. Epigeal B. **Epicotyl**

  C. Epistasis D. Epigyny

- Stripe rust in wheat is due to

  A. *P. graminisrecondita* B. ***P. Graminisstriformis***

  C. *P. graministritici* D. None

- Plant in which the cotyledons appear above the surface of the soil is called as

  A. **Epigeal** B. Epicotyl

  C. Epistasis D. Epigyny

- An alkaloid derived from the *Autumn crocus* that is used as an agent to arrest spindle formation and interrupt mitosis is called as

  A. **Colchicine** B. Proline

  C. Nicotine D. Buteine

- The protective sheath that covers the young shoot of the embryo in plant of the family graminaceae is called as

  A. Endosperm B. **Coleoptile**

  C. protoplast D. Coleorhiza

- Seed lot certificate colour is

  A. Blue B. Green

  C. Purple D. **Orange or green**

- Hot water treatment is used to break dormancy in

  A. **Lentil** B. Cherry

  C. Cotton D. Rice

- Smaller plant virus is

  A. SBYV B. TMV

  C. **Satellite virus** D. PVX

- Radical is enclosed in a protective cover called as

  A. Endosperm B. Coleoptile

  C. Protoplast D. **Coleorhiza**

- The mode of pollination in maize is

  A. **Cross pollination** B. Chasmogamy

  C. Self pollination D. Cliestogamy

- Fruit of castor is called as

  A. Grain B. **Capsule**

  C. Bulb D. Achene

- The white spongy outgrowth of the microphyle present in seeds of castor and tapioca is known as

  A. **Caruncle** B. Capsule

  C. Caryopsis D. Achene

- A dry, indehiscent one seed fruit where the pericarp and inegumENTS are tightly fused to the seed is called as

  A. Caruncle B. Capsule

  C. **Caryopsis** D. Achene

- Gaunch – 1 is variety of

  A. Tomato B. Mango

  C. Bhendi D. **Castor**

- A modified type of spike with a single unisexual flower arising from the peduncle is termed as

  A. **Catkin** B. Capsule

  C. Caryopsis D. Achene

- Pusa snow ball is a variety of the crop is

  A. Tomato B. **Cauliflower**

  C. Bhendi D. Castor

- The progency of the foundation seed, whose production is so handeled to mantain genetic identity and physical purity according to the standards specified for the crop is called as

  A. Breeder seed B. **Certified seed**

  C. Basic seed D. Foundation seed

- The pollination occuring in plants through bats is called

  A. Chasmogamy B. **Cheiropterophily**

  C. Anemophily D. Cliestogamy

- The percent impurity in a seed sample is reffered to as

  A. Admixture B. Roughage

  C. Genetic impurity D. **Dockage**

- Mak - 2 is a variety of

  A. Maize B. Medicage

  C. **Bt cotton** D. Rice

- The phenomenon of a F1 hybrid identical to one of its parent for a characters is termed as

  A. **Dominance** B. Overdominance

  C. Incomplete dominance D. Recessiveness

- The seed which will not germinate under normal environmental conditions is called as

  A. Active seed B. Dead seed

  C. **Dormant seed** D. Regected seed

- The terms that represents the tissue of seed that develops from sexual fusion of the polar nuclei of the ovule and the second male sperm cell is called as

  A. Embryo B. Radicle

  C. **Endosperm** D. Plumule

- A miniature plant which consists of plumule, radicle and cotyledon is called as

  A. **Embryo** B. Grain

  C. Endosperm D. Explant

- Fungi and bacteria usually enters through

  A. **Stomata** B. Wounds

  C. Hydathods D. Insect puncture

- Inflorescence of cauliflower is called as

  A. Spike B. **Curd**

  C. Bulb D. Achene

- A hybrid derived from the fusion of cytoplast of one parent and protoplast of the other parent, contains nucleus from one parent and cytoplast from both the parents is called as

  A. Embryo B. Explant

  C. Hybrid D. **Cybrid**

- An idividual that had more than two complete chromosome sets of a single genome is called as

  A. Hexaploid B. Allopolyploid

  C. Aneuploid D. **Autopolyploid**

- A slender bristle shape, elongated appendage or extension of the glume, achene etc. present in wheat, rye and rice is called as

  A. Spike B. Auricles

  C. **Awns** D. Spikelet

- A cross between a hybrid F^1 or a segregating generation and one of its parents is known as

  A. Monocross B. **Back cross**

  C. Triple cross D. Three way cross

- Coating the seeds with biological agents like bacteria is called as

  A. **Bio-priming** B. Bio-layering

  C. Bio-synthetic D. Bio-nomics

- A population of individuals that have identical genetic but varying physiological characters is known as

  A. Genotype B. Phenotype

  C. Pathotype D. **Biotype**

- The colour of the seed sample certificate is

  A. Yellow B. **Blue**

  C. Green D. Red

- Neurotoxin present in lythyrus is called

  A. OBAA B. AABO

  C. **BOAA** D. ABAO

- The seed, which is produced by a breeder or the institute, which developed the variety and is a source of foundation seed is called

A. **Breeder seed** B. Certified seed

C. Basic seed D. Foundation seed

- Seed coat peroxidase test is used for

A. **Soybean** B. Wheat

C. Sorghum D. Rice

- In paddy, endosperm is separeted by a layer known

A. Silicon layer B. Endothelium

C. Pericarp D. **Epithelium**

- The fatty acids that is specific to the seed oil of brassica spp. is

A. Lactic acid B. Palmatic acid

C. **Erucic acid** D. Crucic acid

- The notified variety or a farmers variety that is in public domain is called

A. Derived variety B. **Extant variety**

C. Farmers variety D. Extint variety

- The variety that has been traditionally cultivated and developed by farmers, or is wild relative or land race in common knowledge of farmers is called

A. Derived variety B. Extant variety

C. **Farmers variety** D. Extint variety

- Pure seed fraction according to seed standards in *Abelmoschusesculentus* should be

A. 98 B. 95

C. **99** D. 93

- The union of male and female gametes in sexual reproduction is known as

  A. **Fertilization** B. Pollination

  C. Infertility D. Incompatibility

- The layer from which hydrolytic enzymes in germinating cereal grain starts from

  A. Meristem layer B. Proline layer

  C. Lysine layer D. **Aleurone layer**

- The presence of male flower in additional to the bisexual flower on different plants is called as

  A. Androtriecious B. **Androdioecious**

  C. Androgynodioecious D. Andromonoecious

- Chromosome constitution different from the usual diploid constitution by loss or duplication of chromosomes or chromosomal segments is called as

  A. Hexaploid B. Allopolyploid

  C. **Aneuploid** D. Autopolyploid

- Shape of starch grain in maize is

  A. Elliptical B. **Angular**

  C. Round D. Square

- The process of dehiscence of anthers and the period of pollen distribution is called as

  A. Antheriosis B. Maturity

  C. Milking D. **Anthesis**

- The process in which seeds are formed but the embryos develop without fertilization is known as

  A. Apogamy B. Apospory

  C. Anagenesis D. **Apomixis**

- The coloured flesh mass present on the outside of the seed in nutmeg is called

  A. **Aril** B. Stigma

  C. Anther D. Endosperm

- Name of the Vitamin - C is known as

  A. Folic acid B. Tocopherol

  C. **Ascorbic acid** D. Riboflavin

- In cereals, grain starch is consists of

  A. Amylopectin B. Amylose

  C. **Both a and b** D. Galactose

- Seed drying is very important to maintain its

  A. **Viability and vigour** B. Oil content

  C. Protein content D. Chemical composition

- New genes are created by

  A. Recombination B. Inversion

  C. **Mutation** D. None

- Possible reasons for seed dormancy is

  A. Presence of pathogens B. **Immature embryo**

  C. Cracking of hulls D. Green distortion

- The outermost wall of the ovary is called as

  A. Mesocarp B. Metacarp

  C. Epicarp D. **Pericarp**

- The tissue of seed that develops from sexual fusion of the polar nuclei of the ovule and the second sperm cell, the term used as

  A. Aril B. Stigma

  C. Anther D. **Endosperm**

- The rudimentary root of the seed or seedling that forms the primary root of the young plant is known as

  A. Rachis B. Recerne

  C. Rachilla D. **Radicle**

- A layer of nutritional tissue of a diploid maternal origin arising from the nucellus and often surrounding the endosperm is called as

  A. Mesosperm B. Metasperm

  C. Episperm D. **Perisperm**

- The appearance of a plant with respect to particular character, such as plant height, flower colour etc., is known as

  A. Genotype B. **Phenotype**

  C. Pathotype D. Biotype

- Occurrence of more than one embryo in seed is known as

  A. Hyperembryony B. Hypoembryony

  C. Heteroembryony D. **Polyembryony**

- Solar treatment is use for

  A. Stem rust B. **Loose smut**

  C. Powdery mildew D. Blast

- Half gram is working sample for purity analysis for

  A. Tomato B. Onion

  C. Berseem D. **Tobacco**

- Certified seed of cotton should have minimum germination of

  A. 50 % B. **60 %**

  C. 70 % D. 80 %

- ISTA was established in the year

A. 1871 B. **1924**

C. 1876 D. 1921

- The first super fine aromatic Basmati hybrid released in India is

A. GEB 24 B. Pusa RH 23

C. **Pusa RH - 10** D. Pusa Basmati 1

- The dwarf variety of rice released in India is

A. IR 8 B. TN - 4

C. **Jaya** D. PR 10

- The average oil content of castor seed is

A. 20 % B. 47 %

C. **26 %** D. 30 %

- National Biodiversity Board in India is situated at

A. Banglore B. New Delhi

C. Mumbai D. **Chennai**

- Crop which has highest unsaturated fatty acid content is

A. **Castor** B. Coconut

C. Linseed D. Niger

- Apical dominance in sugarcane is suppressed by

A. IAA B. ABA

C. GA3 D. **Cytokinins**

- Clove is obtained from

A. **Bud** B. Fruit

C. Flower D. Stem

- The treatment of seeds with an osmotic solution i.e., polyethylene glycol to initiate germination and then dried to get more uniform and rapid germination of certain vegetable seeds is called as

  A. **Priming** B. Stratification

  C. Screening D. Purification

- The seed - bearing structure of conifers consisting of a central stem, woody or scales, bracts, and seeds is termed as

  A. **Cone** B. Bract

  C. Corolla D. Caryopsis

- Death of seeds, germinant or young seedlings in the nursery resulting from attack by certain soil-living fungi is defined as

  A. Rotting B. **Damping - off**

  C. Glotting D. Fermentation

- Group of enzymes catalysing reaction involving transfer of hydrogen from a substrate to a hydrogen acceptor is named as

  A. Glutamase B. Hydrogenase

  C. Methionase D. **Dehydrogenase**

- Extraction of seeds or stones by removal of the fleshy part (pulp) of fruits like berries and drupes is called as

  A. **Depulping** B. Decantation

  C. Pulping D. Pulp decantation

- Sodium hydroxide is the chemical name for

  A. **Caustic soda** B. Salt paper

  C. Caustic potash D. Baking soda

- Triticale is a cross between

  A. Wheat × Rice B. Wheat × Maize

  C. **Wheat × Rye** D. Wheat × Oat

- Sodium carbonate is the chemical name for

  A. Caustic soda B. Salt petre

  C. **Washing soda** D. Baking soda

- Plants adapted to saline soils are called as

  A. Lithophytes B. Xerophytes

  C. Chasmophytes D. **Halophytes**

- Termites is also called as

  A. Red ants B. Black ants

  C. **White ants** D. All of these

- Saffron (kesar) belongs to the family

  A. Lauraceae B. Apiaceae

  C. Orchidaceae D. **Iridaceae**

- The chemical name of Marsh gas is

  A. Ethane B. Ethylene

  C. **Methane** D. Carbon dioxide

- Biurate content in urea is

  A. 1.5 % B. **2.0 %**

  C. 3.0 % D. 5.0 %

- Minute opening in the integument of an ovule through which the pollen grain or pollen tube passes to reach the embryo sac is called as

  A. **Micropyle** B. Auricle

  C. Integument D. Pericarp

- Fungi that produce distinct mycelium or spore mass on the host are called as

  A. Necrosis B. **Mould**

  C. Masting D. Mycorrhiza

- Procedure by which individual seeds are provided with an envelope of adhesive material containing e.g. nutrients, microsymbiont inoculant and/or pesticides is known as

  A. Spike B. Stacking

  C. Crushing D. **Pelleting**

- Collective term for the outer part of flower comprising calyx and corolla is known as

  A. Spike B. **Perianth**

  C. Auricle D. Spikelet

- Region in the ovary where the ovules originate and are attached to the carpel is known as

  A. **Placenta** B. Ligule

  C. Planta D. Auricle

- Many seeded fruit derived from a compound pistil embedded in a fleshy hypanthium or floral tube of epigynous flower is known as

  A. Pod B. Caryopsis

  C. Capsule D. **Pome**

- The most destructive insect in the world is

  A. Termites B. **Desert locusts**

  C. White flies D. None of these above

- The Central Agricultural University is located at

  A. **Manipur** B. Hyderabad

  C. New Delhi D. Chennai

- The chemical name of Milk of Magnesis is

  A. **Magnesium hydroxide** B. Magnesium carbonate

  C. Magnesium chloride D. Magnesium oxide

- End product of glycolysis is

  A. ATP　　B. **Pyruvate**

  C. PEP　　D. None of these

- Phosphorus in plants is absorbed as

  A. PO4　　B. **H2PO4**

  C. SSP　　D. None of these

- Inactive, resting, and applicable to non-dormant seeds during the interval between maturation on the parent tree and the onest of germination is known as

  A. Quinquencial　　B. **Quiescent**

  C. Dessication　　D. Stratification

- Ridge formed on the seed-coat if the funiculus is fused with the integuments in part of its length in anatropous or campylotropous ovules is known as

  A. **Raphe**　　B. Auricle

  C. Ligule　　D. Scales

- An elongate inflorescence with sessile flowers is normally called as

  A. **Racemose**　　B. Sporodix

  C. Spike　　D. None of these

- Simple, indirect test of viability, by which seeds are first allowed to imbibe water and are then squashed with a pair of forceps to reveal the condition of the embryo is called as

  A. Squash test　　B. Hiltner test

  C. **Vilmorin test**　　D. Health test

- Fungi living in symbiosis with plant roots and provides the plant with minerals nutrients and gets in return sugar and other organic compounds is called as

  A. Maceration B. Mould

  C. Masting D. **Mycorrhiza**

- The individual flower stalk in an inforescence is known as

  A. Spikelet B. **Pedicel**

  C. Auricle D. Pelliclle

- The main axis of an inforescence or, in the case of single flower, the flower or fruit stalk is known as

  A. **Peduncle** B. Spikelet

  C. Auricle D. Pellicle

- A seed which can germinate under favourable conditions, provided that any dormancy that may be present is removed is known as

  A. Retained seed B. Synthetic seed

  C. **Viable seed** D. Dead seed

- The seed properties which determine the potential for rapid, uniform emergence and development of normal seedlings under a wide range of field condition is known as

  A. **Vigour** B. Tumbling

  C. Viviparous D. Imbibition

- Seed germinating while still attached to the parent plant, e.g. *Rhizophora* spp and extremely difficult to store are known as

  A. Vigour B. Tumbling

  C. **Viviparous** D. Imbibition

- Isolation distance for foundation seed in hybrid sunflower is

  A. 50 metres B. 100 metres

  C. 1000 metres D. **600 metres**

- IGFRI is located at

  A. **Jhansi** B. Jodhpur

  C. Jaipur D. Jorhat

- The second most abudant element found in earth's crust is

  A. Carbon B. Oxygen

  C. **Silicon** D. Calcium

- In plants, enzyme responsible for the synthesis of the malic acid is

  A. **Rubisco** B. Urease

  C. Carboxylase D. Kinase

- Potassium hydroxide is also known as

  A. Lunar caustic B. Salt petre

  C. **Caustic soda** D. All of these

- Maize belong to the category

  A. Dioecious B. **Monoecious**

  C. Bisexual D. Cliestogamous

- Chemical compound that has a high moisture absorption affinity and can be used for desiccation or maintaining a low humidity when stored together with e. g. seeds, is called as

  A. Extractant B. Humidiant

  C. Absorbant D. **Desiccant**

- Oil - rich outgrowth on seed or fruit which is eaten by ants and thus serves to disperse the seed is called as

  A. Palentosome B. Paleosome

  C. Eloque D. **Elaiosome**

- Method for cleaning seeds from particles with higher or lower specific density by submerging in water or other liquid is called as

  A. Separation　　B. **Flotation**

  C. Desicator　　D. Humidification

- The stalk of an ovule or seed, attaching it to the ovary placenta is called as

  A. Ligule　　B. Peduncle

  C. **Funicle**　　D. Aricle

- A flower that does not open for pollination but is pollinated and fertilised by its own pollen within a closed system is called as

  A. Chasmogamous flower　　B. Monoecious flower

  C. **Cleistogamous flower**　　D. Herkogamous flower

- Mix of several primary samples taken from different parts of a seed lot is called as

  A. Uniform sample　　B. **Composite sample**

  C. Graded sample　　D. Specified sample

- Seed with hard, impermeable seed-coat that prevents imbibition is called

  A. Synthetic seed　　B. Coated seed

  C. **Hard seed**　　D. Dead seed

- Test for the pathogen infection of seed is named as

  A. Patent test　　B. Garden seed

  C. DUS test　　D. **Health test**

- IDS means

  A. **Incubation-desication-separation**

  B. Incubation-deterioration-separation

  C. Insulation-desication-separation

  D. Insulation-deterioration-separation

- The process of the initial water uptake by seed prior to germination is known as

A. Germination B. Desication

C. **Imbibition** D. Impermeation

- The one or two layers (often fused) of tissue covering and surrounding the nucellus of an ovule is called as

A. **Integument** B. Radical

C. Capsule D. Epicarp

- The isolation distance normally followed for foundation seed production of paddy varieties will be

A. **3 metres** B. 10 metres

C. 50 metres D. 1000 metres

- The isolation distance normally followed for foundation seed production of paddy hybrids will be

A. 3 metres B. 50 metres

C. 10 metres D. **200 metres**

- The isolation distance normally followed for foundation seed production of cotton hybrid will be

A. 30 metres B. **50 metres**

C. 100 metres D. 1000 metres

- The maximum moisture content percentage for safe storage in wheat seed is around

A. 18 % B. 24 %

C. 12 % D. **5 %**

- The sugar turn out from cane in India is approximately

A. 24 - 26 % B. **8 - 10 %**

C. 4 - 5 % D. 18 - 20 %

❐ The equipment used to life the seeds to the top of bins/machines for cleaning, sorting or sacking is called as

A. Grader
B. Desiccator
C. **Bucket elevator**
D. Humidifier

❐ Formation of an elongated stem or seed stalk, and occurs generally during the second season of growth in case biennial plants is called as

A. Pome
B. Achene
C. **Bolt**
D. Caryopsis

❐ The sheath which surrounds the primary root in the embryo of grasses is called as

A. Endosperm
B. Coleoptile
C. Protoplast
D. **Coleorhiza**

❐ The test performed to determine the genuineness of seed as to species or variety, or freedom from seed borne infection is called as

A. **Grow out test**
B. Vilmorin test
C. Germination test
D. Vigour test

❐ The chemical name of quick lime is

A. Calcium hydroxide
B. Calcium carbonate
C. Calcium chloride
D. **Calcium oxide**

❐ Mendel worked on

A. Sweet peas
B. Field peas
C. **Garden peas**
D. Beans

❐ The chemical name of soda ash is

A. Sodium hydroxide
B. **Sodium carbonate**
C. Sodium chloride
D. Sodium oxide

- The chemical name of phenol is

  A. Stratosphere B. Methioic acid

  C. Troposphere D. **Carbolic acid**

- Global warming is attributed to increase in concetration of green house gases like

  A. CO2 B. CH4

  C. CFCs D. **All of these**

- The colour of liquid oxygen is

  A. Red B. **Blue**

  C. White D. Green

- In India, the most common method of irrigation crops

  A. Drip B. Sprinkler

  C. **Check basin** D. Border strip

- Potassium nitrate is also known as

  A. Lunar caustic B. **Salt petre**

  C. Caustic potash D. All of these

- The depth of seedling in wheat depends on the lenght of A. Mesocotyle B. Radical

  C. **Coleoptile** D. Plumule

- Silver nitrate is also known as

  A. **Lunar caustic** B. Salt paper

  C. Caustic potash D. All of these

- Soil mulch is useful in

  A. Impoving aeration

  B. Improving drinage

  C. **Minimise evaporation losses**

  D. Removing weeds

- Sodium bicarbonate is the chemical name for

  A. Caustic soda B. Salt petre

  C. Rice D. **Baking soda**

- Crop logging is done in

  A. Maize B. **Sugarcane**

  C. Rice D. Cotton

- Green revolution is related to

  A. Maize & Rice B. Sugarcane & Cotton

  C. **Wheat & Rice** D. Pulses

- Sequence of growing crops on a given piece of land is known as

  A. Crop insurance B. **Crop rotation**

  C. Cropping intensity D. Risk cropping

- The minimum specific heat of water occurs at a temperature of

  A. 0^0C B. 100^0C

  C. **37^0C** D. 50^0C

- The process in which an unfertilized egg can develop into an adult is known as

  A. Parthenocarpy B. Apogamy

  C. **Parthenogenesis** D. Apomixis

- Karnal bunt is a serious disease of

  A. **Wheat** B. Tomato

  C. Apple D. Mango

- In the presence of sunlight, CO2 and H2O (with the help of chlorophyll) and converted into carbohydrates, this process is known as

  A. Respiration B. Metabolism

  C. **Photosynthesis** D. Transpiration

- The net gain of ATP during glycolysis is

  A. **2** B. 6

  C. 4 D. 10

- The plant cells are connected with the help of

  A. Cell wall B. Plasma membrane

  C. Golgi complex D. **Plasmodesmata**

- Oleoresin is an important product of

  A. Potato B. Tomato

  C. **Chilli** D. Cotton

- The gradual loss of variability in the cultivated forms and in their wild relatives is referred to as

  A. Genetic drift B. Genetic shift

  C. **Genetic erosion** D. None of the above

- In crops, grow out test is done for the verification of its trueness to type or variety, which is termed as

  A. **Genetic purity** B. Crop purity

  C. Dockage purity D. Seed purity

- Seed drying is very important to maintain its

  A. **Viability and vigour** B. Oil content

  C. Protein content D. Chemical composition

- New genes are created by

  A. Recombination B. Inversion

  C. **Mutation** D. None

- Possible reasons for seed dormancy is

  A. Presence of pathogens B. **Immature embryo**

  C. Cracking of hulls D. Green distortion

- The average oil content of castor seed is

  A. 20 % B. 47 %

  C. **26 %** D. 30 %

- National Biodiversity Board in India is situated at

  A. Banglore B. New Delhi

  C. Mumbai D. **Chennai**

- Crop which is known as camel crop is

  A. Maize B. Wheat

  C. **Sorghum** D. Pearl Millet

- Crop which has highest unsaturated fatty acid content

  A. **Castor** B. Coconut

  C. Linseed D. Niger

- Apical dominance in sugarcane is suppressed by

  A. IAA B. ABA

  C. GA3 D. **Cytokinins**

- Clove is obtained from

  A. **Bud** B. Fruit

  C. Flower D. Stem

- The phenomenon of a F1 hybrid identical to one of its parent for a character is termed as

  A. **Dominance** B. Overdominance

  C. Incomplete dominance D. Recessiveness

- The seed which will not germinate under normal environmental conditions is called as

  A. Active seed B. Dead seed

  C. **Dormant seed** D. Regected seed

- The terms thet represents the tissue of seed that develops from sexual fusion of the polar nuclei of the ovule and the second male sperm cell is called as

  A. Embryo B. Radicle

  C. **Endosperm** D. Plumule

- A miniature plant which consists of plumule, radicle and cotyledon is called as

  A. **Embryo** B. Grain

  C. Endosperm D. Explant

- Fungi and bacteria usually enters through

  A. **Stomata** B. Wounds

  C. Hydathods D. Insect puncture

- Inflorescence of cauliflower is called as

  A. Spike B. **Curd**

  C. Bulb D. Achene

- A slender bristle shape, elongated appandage or extension of the glume, achene etc. present in wheat, rye and rice is called as

  A. Spike B. Auricles

  C. **Awns** D. Spikelet

- A cross between a hybrid F^1 or a segregating generation and one of its parents is known as

  A. Monocross B. **Back cross**

  C. Triple cross D. Three way cross

- A population of individuals that have identical genetic but varying physiological characters is known as

  A. Genotype B. Phenotype

  C. Pathotype D. **Biotype**

- The colour of the seed sample certificate is

  A. Yellow B. **Blue**

  C. Green D. Red

- The seed, which is produced by a breeder or the institute, which developed the variety and is a source of foundation seed is called

  A. **Breeder seed** B. Certified seed

  C. Basic seed D. Foundation seed

- In paddy, endosperm is separated by a layer known

  A. Silicon layer B. Endothelium

  C. Pericarp D. **Epithelium**

- The fatty acids that is specific to the seed oil of brassica spp. is

  A. Lactic acid B. Palmatic acid

  C. **Erucic acid** D. Crucic acid

- The notified variety or a farmers variety that is in public domain is called

  A. Derived variety B. **Extant variety**

  C. Farmers variety D. Extint variety

- The variety that has been traditionally cultivated and developed by farmers, or is wild relative or land race in common knowledge of farmers is called

  A. Derived variety B. Extant variety

  C. **Farmers variety** D. Extint variety

- The layer from which hydrolytic enzymes in germinating cereal grain starts from

  A. Meristem layer B. Proline layer

  C. Lysine layer D. **Aleurone layer**

- The presence of male flower in additional to the bisexual flower on different plants is called as

A. Androtriecious B. **Androdioecious**

C. Androgynodioecious D. Andromonoecious

- Chromosome constitution different from the usual diploid constitution by loss or duplication of chromosomes or chromosomal segments is called as

A. Hexaploid B. Allopolyploid

C. **Aneuploid** D. Autopolyploid

- Shape of starch grain in maize is

A. Elliptical B. **Angular**

C. Round D. Square

- The process of dehiscence of anthers and the period of pollen distribution is called as

A. Antheriosis B. Maturity

C. Milking D. **Anthesis**

- The process in which seeds are formed but the embryos develop without fertilization is known as

A. Apogamy B. Apospory

C. Anagenesis D. **Apomixis**

- The coloured flesh mass present on the outside of the seed in nutmeg is called

A. **Aril** B. Stigma

C. Anther D. Endosperm

- Seed drying is very important to maintain its

A. **Viability and vigour** B. Oil content

C. Protein content D. Chemical composition

- The tissue of seed that develops from sexual fusion of the polar nuclei of the ovule and the second sperm cell, the term used as

  A. Aril B. Stigma

  C. Anther D. **Endosperm**

- The rudimentary root of the seed or seedling that forms the primary root of the young plant is known as

  A. Rachis B. Recerne

  C. Rachilla D. **Radicle**

- A layer of nutritional tissue of a diploid maternal origin arising from the nucellus and often surrounding the endosperm is called as

  A. Mesosperm B. Metasperm

  C. Episperm D. **Perisperm**

- The appearance of a plant with respect to particular character, such as plant height, flower colour etc., is known as

  A. Genotype B. **Phenotype**

  C. Pathotype D. Biotype

- Occurrence of more than one embryo in seed is known as

  A. Hyperembryony B. Hypoembryony

  C. Heteroembryony D. **Polyembryony**

- Solar treatment is use for

  A. Stem rust B. **Loose smut**

  C. Powdery mildew D. Blast

- Half gram is working sample for purity analysis for

  A. Tomato B. Onion

  C. Berseem D. **Tobacco**

- Certified seed of cotton should have minimum germination of

  A. 50 % B. **60 %**

  C. 70 % D. 80 %

- ISTA was established in the year

  A. 1871 B. **1924**

  C. 1876 D. 1921

- The first super fine aromatic Basmati hybrid released in India is

  A. GEB 24 B. Pusa RH 23

  C. **Pusa RH - 10** D. Pusa Basmati 1

- The dwarf variety of rice released in India is

  A. IR 8 B. TN - 4

  C. **Jaya** D. PR 10

- The average oil content of castor seed is

  A. 20 % B. 47 %

  C. **26 %** D. 30 %

- National Biodiversity Board in India is situated at

  A. Banglore B. New Delhi

  C. Mumbai D. **Chennai**

- Crop which has highest unsaturated fatty acid content is

  A. **Castor** B. Coconut

  C. Linseed D. Niger

- Apical dominance in sugarcane is suppressed by

  A. IAA B. ABA

  C. GA3 D. **Cytokinins**

- Clove is obtained from

  A. **Bud** B. Fruit

  C. Flower D. Stem

- The treatment of seeds with an osmotic solution i.e., polyethylene glycol to initiate germination and then dried to get more uniform and rapid germination of certain vegetable seeds is called as

  A. **Priming** B. Stratification

  C. Screening D. Purification

- The phenomenon of a single major gene affecting more than one character is called as

  A. Pathogenecity B. Inheritance

  C. Plasticity D. **Pleiotrophy**

- The portion of the seed embryo, which produces the aerial portion, which develops into a plant is called as

  A. Embryo B. Radical

  C. Endosperm D. **Plumul**

- The transfer of pollen from the anther to the stigma of the flower is known as

  A. Emasculation B. **Pollination**

  C. Detasselling D. Tasseling

- Along the following plant which one does not show photorespiration

  A. Rice B. Wheat

  C. **Maize** D. Pea

- How many Agricultural Universities are there presently in India?

  A. 35 B. **47**

  C. 8 D. 31

- Vegetable rich in vitamin - C is

  A. **Capsicum** B. Beetroot

  C. Tomato D. Wheat

- Triticale has been developed by crossing wheat with

  A. Barley B. Phalaris

  C. **Rye** D. Bajra

- Green Revolution started in India in the year

  A. **1964** B. 1969

  C. 1961 D. 1974

- *Corchrus capsularis* is the botanical name of which plant ?

  A. Rice B. Sunhemp

  C. **Jute** D. Cotton

- Dicot endospermic seed is

  A. Castor B. Fenugreek

  C. **Both a and b** D. Bean

- In India, normally how many generation system seed are produced ?

  A. 2 B. **3**

  C. 1 D. 4

- The leathery cartilaginous covering of a seed as in mango can be termed as

  A. **Putamen** B. Pericarp

  C. Cartilage D. Ligule

- The condition in which the seed germination is prevented by the absence of the basic conditions required for the normal germination and growth is called as

  A. Dormancy B. **Quiuescence**

  C. Dead seed D. Proactive seed

- The equipment used to apply chemical that involves suspension and wettable powder treatment material in water is

  A. **Slurry treaters** B. Panogen treaters

  C. Direct treaters D. Mist-o-matic treaters

- The two most important factors influencing the life span of seed under storage are

  A. **RH and temperature** B. Climate and temperature

  C. Rainfall and RH D. Seed size and moisture content

- Indian Seed Act was enacted in the year

  A. **1966** B. 1959

  C. 1953 D. 1975

- Cross pollination in Bajra occurs due to

  A. Protoandry B. **Protogyny**

  C. Cleistogamy D. Chasmogamy

- The inflorescence of wheat is called as

  A. Racemose B. Sporodix

  C. **Spike** D. None of these

- Gibberellic acid was first isolated from

  A. **Fungus** B. Minerals

  C. Animals D. Bacteria

- Wheat protein is called as

  A. Zein B. **Gluten**

  C. Ricin D. Durin

- Germination is inhibited by

  A. Red light B. Blue light

  C. **IR light** D. UV light

- Epigeal germination is found in

  A. pea B. Gram

  C. **Cucumber** D. Mango

- Which is the total root parasite

  A. Orabanche B. Conophalis

  C. Epitagus D. **All**

- The name of the protein, which is much useful in varietal identification

  A. Tocophenol B. **Prolamine**

  C. ABA D. Auxin

- Shape of the starch grain in barley is

  A. Elliptical B. **Spherical**

  C. Granulated D. Round

- The type of sowing that is normally practiced to obtained synchronized flowering during hybrid seed production is called as

  A. Line sowing B. Spherical sowing

  C. **Staggered sowing** D. Isolated sowing

- In groundnut, the process of removing the pods either mechanically/manually is known as

  A. Stacking B. Removing

  C. **Stripping** D. Roughing

- Sexual function of the sperm and egg cell is called as

  A. **Syngamy** B. Exogamy

  C. Synteny D. Dichogamy

- Process of bringing grains or other products to a desired moisture or temperature for processing is called

  A. **Tempering** B. Grading

  C. Processing D. Stacking

- The outer layer of the seed coat which is smooth and rough is known as

  A. Lerma B. Palea

  C. **Testa** D. Glume

- Uptake of water from the atmosphere by cells or tissue in the seed-coat is called as

  A. Wetting of the seed B. Adsorption

  C. Adhesion D. **Absorption**

- One - seeded, dry, indehiscent fruit, formed from one carpel is called

  A. Caryopsis B. Sorosis

  C. **Achene** D. Capsule

- The taking up of one substance at the surface of another, e.g. adhesion of a liquid or a substrate on a seed-coat is called

  A. Wetting of the seed B. **Adsorption**

  C. Adhesion D. Absorption

- Progression of cytological and biochemical events which ultimately leads to the death of the seed is defined as

  A. **Ageing** B. Activation
  C. Germination D. Death progression

- Many - seeded fruit derived from an *apocarpous* overy in which the pistils from individual simple fruits which may be separate or fused with each other and the receptacle is called

  A. **Albumen** B. Protein
  C. Globulin D. Glutenin

- Ovule orientation in which the ovule is inverted with respect to its funiculus is known as

  A. Exotropous ovule B. **Anatropous ovule**
  C. Inverted ovule D. Exerted ovule

- Ovule where the microphyle is oriented at an angle to the placenta is called as

  A. Anacardous fruit B. Capsule
  C. Tropic fruit D. **Campylotropous**

- Region in the ovule opposite the micropyle where the integuments fuse with funiculus is called as

  A. **Caruncle** B. Ligule
  C. Chalaza D. Endosperm

- The vitamin, which is responsible for embryo and endosperm development is called as

  A. Glutamine B. Protein
  C. **Thiamine** D. Auxin

- The cross between a single cross hybrid (A x B) and inbred (C) is termed as

  A. **Three way cross** B. Double cross
  C. Single cross D. Poly cross

- The ability of a plant cell to develop into a complete plant is called as

  A. **Totiopotency** B. Probability

  C. Prepotency D. Pureline effect

- Central Potato Research Station is situated at

  A. Banglore B. **Shimla**

  C. Almora D. Shillong

- The seed which show very drastic loss in viability with a decrease in moisture content below 12 to 13 % are called

  A. Dead seed B. Obsolete seed

  C. **Recalcitrant seed** D. Calcitrant seed

- The culture by which the legume seeds are to be inoculated before sowing in the new area is called

  A. Trichogramma B. Azosprillus

  C. Azatobacter D. **Rhizobium**

- The removal of off-type plant i.e., plants phenotypically different from the plant of a variety under certification from a seed crop is called

  A. **Rouging** B. Distribution

  C. Grading D. Burning

- The physical or chemical process that weakens or softens seed coat is known as

  A. Stratification B. Centrification

  C. **Scarification** D. Vitrification

- The direct and immediate visible effect of the foreign pollen on the seed coat colour during the formation of seed is called as

  A. Fertilized effect B. Pollen impact

  C. **Xenia** D. Penetrance

- The name of the father of the hybrid rice is

  A. M. S. Swaminathan B. Tia Zhung

  C. **Yuan Long Ping** D. Borlaug Norman

- The first cytokinin identified in plants is called as

  A. **Zeatin** B. Protein

  C. Glutenin D. Lycopene

- The percentage of amylase present in a starch grain is nearly

  A. 1 – 2 % B. 40 – 45 %

  C. **20 – 25 %** D. 38 -42 %

- Which one of the following is the biochemical deterioration of seed?

  A. Loss of weight B. **Free radical production**

  C. Loss of germination D. Loss of vigour

- The first generation resulting from crossing of two inbreds is

  A. **Hybrid** B. Synthesis

  C. Composites D. Variety

- The first generation resulting from the controlled crossing of an approved inbred line and open pollinated variety is

  A. Single cross B. Double cross

  C. **Top cross** D. Four way cross

- The cross between parents differing in a single gene is

  A. Double hybrid B. **Mono hybrid**

  C. Single cross hybrid D. Triple cross hybrid

- The superiority of an F1 hybrid over both its parents in terms of yield and some other characters is defined as

  A. Inbreeding depression B. **Heterosis**

  C. Clonal degeneration D. Heterobeltiosis

- The progency obtained by hybridization between two or more genetically dissimilar individuals, strains, pure, lines etc., is called as

  A. Embryo B. Explant

  C. Cybrid D. **Hybrid**

- The reduction or loss in vigour and fertility as a result of inbreeding is called as

  A. Heritability B. **Inbreeding depression**

  C. Heterosis D. Cybrid line

- Progeny of a single homozygous plant of a self pollinated species is called as

  A. Dihybrid B. **Pure line**

  C. Inbred D. Monohybrid

- The variety produced by crossing in all combination of a number of lines that combine well with each other is called as

  A. Varietal mixtures B. Hybrid variety

  C. Composite variety D. **Synthetic variety**

- The male sterile parent is crossed with one of the following line to produce hybrid line

  A. A line B. B line

  C. **R line** D. C line

- Hybrid rice seed production is carried out by

  A. One line system B. Multi line system

  C. **Three line system** D. Four line system

- The first generation progeny of a cross between two single cross hybrids

  A. Single cross hybrid B. **Double cross hybrid**

  C. Back cross hybrid D. Three way cross hybrid

- A line become homozygous by repeated selfing upto

  A. 3 generations B. 5 generations

  C. **8 generations** D. 12 generations

- The first developed hormone is

  A. ABA B. CKs

  C. **Auxin** D. GA3

- The major 'auxin' in developing seed is

  A. **IAA** B. ABA

  C. BOAA D. BOA

- Gibberellic acid was first isolated from

  A. **Fungus** B. Minerals

  C. Animals D. Bacteria

- Uptake of water from the atmosphere by cells or tissue in the seed coat is called as

  A. Wetting of the seed B. Adsorption

  C. Adhesion D. **Absorption**

- Impaired viability caused by exposure to low temperature is called as

  A. Drought injury B. **Chilling injury**

  C. Mechanical injury D. Chilling tolerance

- The process of initial water uptake by seeds prior to germination is known as

  A. Germination B. Desiccation

  C. **Imbibition** D. Impermeation

- Seeds which require light are called

  A. Skotoblastic B. **Photo blastic**

  C. Hydrophilic D. Hydrophobic

- One of the requirement for seed germination is

  A. Soil B. **Water**

  C. Fertilizer D. Seed

- The respiration stimulant in germination of seed is

  A. KNO3 B. GA3

  C. **H2O2** D. Thiourea

- Optimum temperature for Brussels sprouts germination

  A. **10-30 degree Celsius** B. 20-40 degree Celsius

  C. 30-50 degree Celsius D. 40-60 degree Celsius

- The emergence of seedling from seed is called as

  A. **Germination** B. Dormancy

  C. Senescence D. Vigour

- The type of germination in onion is

  A. Hypogeal B. **Epigeal**

  C. Semi hypogeal D. Semi epigeal

- Imbibition is a

  A. Chemical process B. **Physical process**

  C. Physiochemical process D. Biochemical process

- The first event in seed germination is

  A. **Imbibition** B. Enzyme activity

  C. Respiration D. Hydrolysis

- Respiration is essential for

  A. AMP production B. ADP production

  C. NADPH production D. **ATP production**

- Which hormone comes under shock hormone

  A. Auxin B. **GA3**

  C. ABA D. SA3

- Which hormone used in growth promoter hormone

  A. **Auxin** B. GAs

  C. ABA D. SAs

- GA synthesis and signaling dominate the transition of

  A. Dormancy B. Sensitivity

  C. **Germination** D. Receptivity

- The seed which will not germinate under normal environmental condition is called as

  A. Live seed B. Dead seed

  C. **Dormant seed** D. Rejected seed

- In paddy, endosperm is separated by a layer is known as

  A. Silicon layer B. Endothelium

  C. Pericarp D. **Epithelium**

- Dormancy caused due to dark is called

  A. Photo dormancy B. Thermo dormancy

  C. **Skoto dormancy** D. Innate dormancy

- Scientist associated with seed dormancy

  A. **Nikolaeva** B. Bewley

  C. Khan D. Roberts

- The plant product which is used to break the dormancy

  A. **Strigol** B. Kharanjia

  C. Pongamol D. Nimbicidin

- Hard seeds are mainly accruing in the family of

  A. **Malvaceae** B. Solanaceae

  C. Rootaceae D. Umbelliferae

- The hard seed coat can be removed by

  A. **Acid scarification** B. After ripening

  C. Drying D. Stratification

- Phytochrome receptor present in

  A. Mitochondria B. Nucleus

  C. Cytoplasm D. **Plasma membrane**

- The type of seed dormancy in *Acacia nilotica* is

  A. **Physiological** B. Physiological

  C. Morphophysiological D. Morphological

- Stratification is given to seed for

  A. Disease resistant

  B. **Dormancy breaking**

  C. Increasing vigour

  D. Creating moisture stress resistance

- Suspension of germination by unfavorable environmental condition is called as

  A. Dormancy B. Embryo dormancy

  C. **Quiescence** D. Resting period

- Fruit of castor is called as

  A. Grain B. Achene

  C. Bulb D. **Capsule**

- The protective sheath that covers the young shoot of the embryo in plants of the family graminaceae is called as

  A. Endosperm B. **Coleoptile**

  C. Protoplast D. Coleorhiza

- Radical is enclosed in a protective cover called as

  A. Endosperm B. Coleoptile

  C. Protoplast D. **Coleorhiza**

- A miniature plant which consists of plumule, radical and cotyledon is called as

  A. **Embryo** B. Aleurone layer

  C. Endosperm D. Perisperm

- The growing point of the embryo which gives rise to the shoot or the above ground part of the plan can be termed as

  A. Epigeal B. **Epicotyl**

  C. Epistasis D. Epigyny

- Plant in which the cotyledon appear above the surface of the soil is called as

  A. **Epigeal** B. Epicotyle

  C. Epistasis D. Epigyny

- The fruit derived from one carpel and splitting along one side is called as

  A. Spike B. Achene

  C. Caryopsis D. **Follicle**

- Each ovule is attached to the placenta by a distinct stalk known as

  A. Embryo B. Radicle

  C. **Hilum** D. Plumule

- The part of the embryo or seedling below the cotyledonary node and above the root is called as

A. Hilum B. **Hypocotyle**

C. Radicle D. Plumule

- The point where the integuments meet at the nucellar apex has been known as

A. Radicle B. Hypocotyle

C. Hilum D. **Microphyle**

- The outmost wall of the ovary is called as

A. Mesocarp B. Metacarp

C. Epicarp D. **Pericarp**

- The rudimentary root of the seed or seedling that forms the primary root of the young plant is known as

A. Embryo B. Recerne

C. Endosperm D. **Radicle**

- A layer of nutritional tissue of a diploid material origin arising from the nucleus and often surrounding the endosperm is called as

A. Mesosperm B. Metasperm

C. Episperm D. **Perisperm**

- Highest protein content is found in

A. Rajmash B. **Soybean**

C. Gram D. Mung bean

- The area between chalaza and hilum in the ovule is known as

A. **Raphae** B. Nucleus

C. Micropyle D. Funicle

- Longest seed viability period of lotus seeds in soil seed bank is

A. 1 years B. 10 years

C. 100 years D. **1000 years**

- Transient seed banks have viability

  A. **1 years** B. 10 years

  C. 100 years D. 1000 years

- Largest seed in the plant kingdom

  A. *Linum usitatissimum* B. *Lactuca sativa*

  C. ***Ladoicea maldivica*** D. *Lactuca scariola*

- Single seeded fruit where pericarp can be removed from the mature seed is called as

  A. **Caryopsis** B. Schizocarp

  C. Achene D. Nut

- An example for monocotyledonous exalbuminous seed

  A. Rice B. **Onion**

  C. Sorghum D. Maize

- Presence of mericarp is common feature of the family

  A. Compositae B. Malvaceae

  C. Solanaceae D. **Umbelliferaceae**

- A seed having little or no endosperm but a well developed perisperm

  A. **Albuminous seed** B. Exalbuminous seed

  C. Endospermous seed D. Non endospermous seed

- A specialized thin tissue which covers the radicle is known as

  A. Root cap B. **Coleorhiza**

  C. Coleoptile D. Nucleus

- The major storage protein of wheat and maize

  A. **Prolamin** B. Albumin

  C. Vicin D. Legumin

- A pore present in the seed coat through which water enters in the seed is known as

  A. Gynaphore B. **Micropyle**

  C. Chalaza D. Synergids

- What is the major storage organ in plant

  A. Endosperm B. **Cotyledon**

  C. Aleurone layer D. Perisperm

- What is the major form of carbohydrate involved in translocation in plants

  A. Starch B. Glucose

  C. Hemi-cellulose D. **Sucrose**

- Small integument out growth is called as

  A. Caruncle B. **Aril**

  C. Hairs D. Elaeiosome

- Anatomically elaeiosome are

  A. Appendages B. Seed coat

  C. **Third cotyledon** D. Embryo

- Seeds with little variability in size and shape are called as

  A. **Euryopermous** B. Cleistogamous

  C. Apomixis D. Stenospermous

- In gymnospermous seeds, the food is stored in

  A. Cotyledon B. Seed coat

  C. Embryo D. **Megagametophyte**

- Orchid seeds are devoid of

  A. Embryo B. Seed coat

  C. Cotyledon D. **Endosperm**

- Perisperm is

  A. Haploid | B. **Diploid**
  C. Tetrapolid | D. Hexapolid

- Which seed content starchy endosperm

  A. Rice | B. Maize
  C. **Sorghum** | D. Pearl millet

- The respiratory quotient in the deteriorated seed is

  A. **High** | B. Low
  C. Medium | D. Absent

- The protein content of wheat is

  A. 10-12 % | B. **10-14 %**
  C. 10-16 % | D. 10-18 %

- The carbohydrate content of maize is

  A. **80-82 %** | B. 60-64 %
  C. 80-86 % | D. 60-68 %

- Albumin is soluble in

  A. **Water** | B. Saline
  C. Alcohol | D. Dilute alkali

- Prolamines are soluble in

  A. Water | B. Dilute alkali
  C. **Alcohol** | D. Saline

- What is the calorific value of carbohydrate seed

  A. **4000** | B. 5000
  C. 5700 | D. 9500

- The major protein content of wheat seed is

  A. Albumin B. Globulin

  C. **Glutelin** D. Prolamin

- Internal component of cell is

  A. Cytoplasm B. **Protoplasm**

  C. Nucleus D. Nucleolus

- The water is taken through the cell wall

  A. Symplastically B. **Apoplastically**

  C. Transcelluar D. Stachyose

- Halum cutting in potato is adopted to avoid

  A. **Viral disease** B. Bacterial disease

  C. Genetic contamination D. Physical contamination

- Miniature plant of the seed is

  A. Plumule B. Radicle

  C. Cotyledons D. **Embryo**

- Food material is supplied to embryo in monocot through

  A. **Scutellum** B. Plumule

  C. Radicle D. Coleoptile

- When the central seed certification board was formed?

  A. 1982 B. **1972**

  C. 1962 D. 1952

- When the seed control order was passed?

  A. **1983** B. 1973

  C. 1963 D. 1953

- The quantity of quality seed that have replaced the actual need of seed

  A. Seed multiplication rate B. **Seed replacement rate**

  C. Seed rate D. Seed yield

- Basic input of agriculture is

  A. Irrigation B. Fertilizer

  C. Soil D. **Seed**

- The progeny of foundation seed is

  A. Nucleus seed B. Breeder seed

  C. **Certified seed** D. Registered seed

- Foundation seed is the progeny of

  A. Truthfully labeled seed B. Foundation seed stage 1

  C. Nucleus seed D. **Breeder seed**

- Breeder seed is the progeny of

  A. Foundation seed B. Breeder seed

  C. **Nucleus seed** D. Certified seed

- Mechanical mixtures commonly occur at the time of

  A. **Sowing** B. Seedling stage

  C. Flowering D. Pod formation stage

3

Biotechnology & Biochemistry

- A small number of improved varieties of each crop become predominant and rapidly replace the heterogeneous local varieties leading to a rapid depletion of genetic variability is called

  i. Genetic depletion ii. **Genetic erosion**

  iii. Genetic vulnerability iv. None of above

- Due to similarity in genotype, the susceptibility of most of the cultivated varieties of a crop species to a disease, insect pest or some other stress is called

  i. Genetic depletion ii. Genetic erosion

  iii. **Genetic vulnerability** iv. None of above

- Noblisation of Indian canes was achieved by

  i. R.B.Singh

  ii. **C.A. Barber, T.S. Venkatraman and others**

  iii. Patrick Shireff

  iv. None of above

- New plants arise from embryos develop without fertilization is called

  i. **Apomixis** ii. Apomeiosis

  iii. Vegetative reproduction iv. None of above

- Embryo developed from egg cell is called

  i. Androgenesis ii. Somatic pseudogamy

  iii. **Gonial pseudogamy** iv. None of above

- Pollen from a flower of one plant falls onto stigma of other flowers of the same plant leading to

  i. **Geitonogamy** ii. Allogamy

  iii. Autogamy iv. None of above

- Chasmogamy is occurs in

  i. Some species in which flowers do not open at all

  ii. **Some species in which flowers open but only after pollination has taken place**

  iii. Both of species

  iv. None of above

- Self-incompatibility was first reported by

  i. **Koelreuter** ii. Gowers

  iii. Lewis iv. None of above

- In Primula flowers with long style and short stemens are called

  i. Thrum flowers ii. **Pin flowers**

  iii. Flowers iv. None of above

- In pollen the incompatibility reaction may be controlled by the genotype of the plant on which it is produced is called

  i. Gametophytic Control ii. **Sporophytic control**

  iii. Both of the above iv. None of above

- Isolation of self-fertile mutations is

  i. Used for gametophytic Control

  ii. **Used toeliminate self-incompatibility**

  iii. Used to eliminate self-compatibility

  iv. None of above

- Self-pollination leads to rapid increase in

  i. Heterozygosity ii. **Homozygosity**

  iii. Both of the above iv. None of above

- The male sterility where the pollen development is normal but pollen function is impaired is called

  i. **Functional male sterility** ii. Sporogenous male sterility

  iii. Structural male sterility iv. None of above

- The gene expression affected little by the prevailing environment is called

  i. Environment sensitive male sterility

  ii. **Environmental insensitive male sterility**

  iii. Both of the above

  iv. None of above

- The male sterile cytoplasms have generally originated through spontaneous mutation in

  i. Self-pollinated crop species

  ii. **Cross pollinated crop species**

  iii. Both of the above

  iv. None of above

- The phenotypic variation in a pureline is due to the

  i. Genetic basis ii. **Environment**

  iii. Both of the above iv. None of above

- The concept of pureline was proposed by

  i. **Johannsen** ii. Comstock and Moll

  iii. Mendel iv. None of above

- Linkage between genes does not affect

  i. **Homozygosity** ii. Heterozygosity

  iii. Both of the above iv. None of above

- Improvement in the mean genotypic value of the selected families over that of the base population is known as

  i. Genetic improvement under selection

  ii. **Genetic advance under selection**

  iii. Both of the above

  iv. None of above

- Realized heritability is

  i. Genetic improvement brought about by mutation

  ii. **Genetic improvement brought about by selection**

  iii. Both of the above

  iv. None of above

- The objective of selfing is

  i. **To avoid cross pollination and to ensure self-pollination**

  ii. To avoid self-pollination and to ensure cross-pollination

  iii. To ensure both self and cross-pollination

  iv. None of above

- Emasculation is

  i. To enclose the flowers or the inflorescences in suitable bags of appropriate size to prevent random cross pollination

  ii. **Removal of stamens or anthers or killing of pollen grains of a flower without affecting in any way the female reproductive organ**

  iii. Both

  iv. None of above

- Hybrid necrosis is

  i. **Discolouration and drying of leaves, which begins at the tips of older leaves and progresses towards their base**

  ii. Discolouration and drying of roots, which begins at the tips of older leaves and progresses towards their base

  iii. Both the above

  iv. None of above

- In evolutionary forces factors involved are

  i. Mutation and selection

  ii. Random drift and Migration

  iii. **Both of the above**

  iv. None of above

- Mating between individuals sharing a common parent in their ancestry is called

  i. Migration ii. **Inbreeding**

  iii. Migration iv. Random drift

- A random change in gene frequency due to sampling error is called

  i. Migration ii. Inbreeding

  iii. Migration iv. **Random drift**

- Mating between individuals, which are phenotypically more similar than would be expected under random mating is called

  i. Genetic disassortative mating

  ii. Phenotypic disassortative mating

  iii. **Phenotypic assortative mating**

  iv. Phenotypic assortative mating

❐ Genetic variability that is available for selection to act on is called

i. **Free genetic variability**

ii. Potential genetic variability

iii. Heterozygotic potential variability

iv. None of the above

❐ The superiority of an F_1 hybrid over both of its parents in terms of yield or some other character is called

i. **Heterosis** ii. Luxuriance

iii. Both iv. None of the above

❐ The heterosis occurs due to over-dominance gene action i.e. superiority of heterozygotes over both the corresponding homozygotes is called

i. **Balanced heterosis** ii. Useful heterosis

iii. Mutational heterosis iv. None of the above

❐ The heterosis which is results from dominance gene action is masking of the deleterious effects of recessive mutant alleles by their dominant counterparts is called

i. **Mutational heterosis** ii. Useful heterosis

iii. Balanced heterosis iv. None of the above

❐ In seed certification programme variety developed by mass selection are

i. Lesser difficult to identify than pureline varieties

ii. **More difficult to identify than pureline varieties**

iii. Both

iv. None of the above

- A large number of plants of similar phenotype are selected and their seeds are mixed together to constitute the new variety is called

  i. **Mass selection**

  ii. Pure line selection

  iii. Both

  iv. None of the above

- A large number of plants are selected from a self pollinated crop and harvested individually, individual plant progenies from them are evaluated, and the best progeny is released as a

  i. Mass selection variety ii. **Pure line variety**

  iii. Both iv. None of the above

- Purelines become genetically variable with time due to

  i. Mechanical mixture ii. Natural hybridization

  iii. Mutation iv. **All of above**

- Malviya Vilalp (MA3) a variety of pigeonpea is an example of

  i. Mass selection ii. **Pureline selection**

  iii. Both iv. None of the above

- MA3 is resistant to

  i. Pigeonpea sterility virus ii. Wilt

  iii. Podfly iv. **All of the above**

- The possibility of commercial utilization of synthetic varieties in maize was first suggested by

  i. Garber ii. Hayes

  iii. **Both** iv. None of the above

- The varieties produced by mixing seeds from several lines or populations of diverse genetic origin are called

  i. Composite variety ii. **Germplasm complexes**

  iii. Both iv. None of the above

- Synthetic varieties can be produced in

  i. Self pollinated crop species

  ii. **Cross pollinated crop species**

  iii. Both

  iv. None of the above

- Hybrid varieties can be produced in

  i. Self pollinated crop species

  ii. Cross pollinated crop species

  iii. **Both**

  iv. None of the above

- The decrease in Syn_2 generation would depend upon

  i. The number of parental lines (Syn_0 populations) constituting the synthetic

  ii. On the difference in yielding abilities of Syn_1 and Syn_0 generations

  iii. **Both**

  iv. None of the above

- Genetic variation within clones may arise due to

  i. Somatic mutation

  ii. Mechanical mixture

  iii. Occasional sexual reproduction

  iv. **All of the above**

- A mutant allele would be homozygous only when
  - i. Both the copies of a gene present in a cell mutate at the same time to produce the same mutant allele
  - ii. The mutant allele is already present in the heterozygous condition in the original clone
  - iii. **In both cases**
  - iv. Never possible

- The main problems peculiar to clonal crops
  - i. Reduced flowering and fertility
  - ii. Difficulties in genetic analysis
  - iii. Perennial life cycle
  - iv. **All the above**

- The strategy of conventional or traditional breeding approaches is
  - i. To select for yield
  - ii. To correct a specific defect
  - iii. **Either i or ii**
  - iv. None of the above

- The term ideotype was introduced by
  - i. Donald 1962
  - ii. **Donald 1968**
  - iii. Beaven 1914
  - iv. Donald 1976

- An ideotype where performance is measured as grain yield per hectare is called
  - i. **Crop ideotype**
  - ii. Competition ideotype
  - iii. Isolation ideotype
  - iv. None of the above

- Salinity tolerance, mineral toxicity/deficiency tolerance are example of
  - i. Stress ideotype
  - ii. **Edaphic ideotype**
  - iii. Disease ideotype
  - iv. Climate ideotype

- Yield is not used as a basis of selection; selection is based on the traits constituting the ideotype in

  i. **Ideotype breeding** ii. Traditional breeding

  iii. Both iv. None of the above

- The trait which has actual usefulness of the produce when consumed by experimental animals; their usefulness to human is usually predicted on this basis is

  i. **Biological quality traits**

  ii. Organoleptic quality traits

  iii. Morphological quality test

  iv. Nutritional quality traits

- Mutation produced by changes in the base sequence of genes is called

  i. **Point mutation** ii. Chromosomal mutation

  iii. Cytoplasmic mutation iv. Somatic mutation

- The mutation which occur in natural populations at a low rate (without any human intervention) is called

  i. **Spontaneous mutation** ii. Induced mutation

  iii. Both iv. None of the above

- When a purine is replaced by another purine then the situation is called as

  i. **Transition** ii. Transversion

  iii. Base substitution iv. None of the above

- Exposure over long periods of time is called

  i. **Chronic exposure** ii. Acute exposure

  iii. Both iv. None of the above

- When the whole L1, L2 or L3 layers of shoot tip meristem is affected by mutagenic treatment, the chimaera is known as

  i. **Periclinal chimaera** ii. Sectorial chimaera

  iii. Both iv. None of the above

- World's first mutant variety is

  i. **Cotton variety MA-9** ii. Cotton variety MCU7

  iii. Cotton variety MCU10 iv. None of the above

- Individuals carrying chromosome number other than the diploid (2x and not 2n) number are called

  i. **Heteropliods** ii. Haploids

  iii. Euploids iv. None of the above

- When an individual has an extra pair of chromosomes is known as

  i. **Tetrasomic** ii. Trisomic

  iii. Double monosomic iv. None of the above

- An Allopolyploid that has two copies of each genome present in it, and behaves essentially as a diploid during meiosis is called

  i. **Amphidiploid** ii. Segmental allopolyploid

  iii. Autopolyploid iv. None of the above

4

Environmental Science

Multiple Choice Based Questions and Answers

- World's largest energy source (at present) is

  i. **Oil** ii. Coal

  iii. Natural gas iv. Solar

- Average ash content of Indian coal is

  i. 70% ii. 60%

  iii. 50% iv. **40%**

- Biggest coal reserve is present in which state

  i. Uttar Pradesh ii. **Jharkhand**

  iii. Bihar iv. Madhya Pradesh

- Maximum damage of plant is caused by pollutant

  i. NO_2 ii. SO_2

  iii. **Both i and ii** iv. SPM

- The process vitrification is used to

  i. **Immobilise nuclear waste**

  ii. Dispose nuclear waste

  iii. Concentrate nuclear waste

  iv. Convert nuclear waste into brick

- Which one of the following is not a biogas energy source?

  i. **Coal** ii. Biogas

  iii. Agricultural residue iv. Municipal wastes

- Ocean is the source of which nuclear fuel?
  i. Tritium ii. **Deuterium**
  iii. Plutonium iv. Thorium

- Promising source of liquid hydrocarbon (as a liquid fuel)
  i. Liliaceae ii. Asclepidaceae
  iii. Euphorbiaceae iv. **Both ii and iii**

- India is huge source of
  i. **Thorium** ii. Uranium
  iii. Deuterium iv. Plutonium

- Most abundant fossil fuel
  i. Oil ii. **Coal**
  iii. Natural gas iv. Peat

- Which among the following region/country produces highest natural gas
  i. USA ii. Middle East
  iii. France iv. **Former USSR**

- The biggest world's primary energy source
  i. **Fossil fuel** ii. Nuclear power
  iii. Coal iv. Hydropower

- The country consume highest per capita energy source is
  i. USA ii. Japan
  iii. Britain iv. **Germany**

- Which industry release spent wash?
  i. Electroplating ii. Pulp and paper
  iii. Tannery iv. **Distillery**

- Phytoremediation is

  i. **Use of plants to remove toxicants from water or soil**

  ii. Use of root mycorrhizae for bioremediation purposes

  iii. Removal of toxicants from plant body by chemical means

  iv. Protection of plants from pests by IPM

- In India major indoor pollutant is

  i. Radon ii. **CO**

  iii. Formaldehyde iv. Ozone

- In motor vehicle catalytic converter can't convert

  i. Hydrocarbon to CO_2 ii. CO to CO_2

  iii. **SO_2 to sulphur** iv. NO_x to N_2

- To control fine particulate emission most suitable scrubber is

  i. **Ventury scrubber** ii. Mechanical scrubber

  iii. Spray tower iv. Packed tower

- In urban area photochemical smog is formed mainly due to

  i. Fog and smoke

  ii. Particulates and fog

  iii. **O_3, PAN and nitrogen oxide**

  iv. Winter climate and high humidity

- Scientific name of White rot fungus used to degrade lignin line complex substrate is

  i. *Trichoderma chrysosporium*

  ii. ***Phanerochaete chrysosporium***

  iii. *Chrysosporium ressi*

  iv. *Penicillium ressi*

- Aerosols are

  i. **Small liquid or solid particles that remain suspended in the air**

  ii. Smoke particles floating in the atmosphere

  iii. Small liquid particles suspended in air

  iv. Small solid particles suspended in air

- Atomic absorption spectrophotometer is used to detect and analyse

  i. Dissolved organic components

  ii. Dissolved gases

  iii. **Heavy elements**

  iv. Particle size

- Source of Byssinosis is

  i. **Textile industry** ii. Rock mine

  iii. Galvanising industry iv. Mica mines

- Workers of coal mines suffers from

  i. Siderosis ii. **Black lung disease**

  iii. Byssinosis iv. Necrosis

- Secondary pollutant is

  i. CH_4 ii. CFCs

  iii. **PAN** iv. CO

- The coldest zone of a lake during summer is

  i. Epilimnon ii. **Hypolimnon**

  iii. Thermolimnon iv. Mesolimnon

- Ganga flows through how many number of states?

  i. 2 ii. 3

  iii. **4** iv. 5

- Tannery effluent contains toxic heavy metal

  i. **Cr** ii. Zn

  iii. Ni iv. Pb

- Commonly used method for sewage treatment in India is

  i. Trickling filter ii. Oxidation pond

  iii. **Activated sludge process** iv. Rotating biological contactor

- Knock knee syndrome is due to

  i. Arsenic toxicity ii. **Fluoride toxicity**

  iii. Cadmium toxicity iv. Lead toxicity

- Carcinogens adversely affect

  i. Cell wall ii. **DNA**

  iii. Cell membrane iv. Mitochondria

- In body tissue DDT accumulates in

  i. Muscles ii. Bone

  iii. Blood iv. **Fat**

- The national forest policy was accepted in

  i. **1952** ii. 1972

  iii. 1974 iv. 1986

- COD is always

  i. Lower than BOD

  ii. Equal to BOD

  iii. **Equal to or higher than BOD**

  iv. 1.8 times of BOD

- For stratospheric ozone depletion the major culprit is

  i. CFCs ii. **Cl radical**

  iii. F radical iv. N_2O

- "Ecology" the term was first proposed by

  i. E. Odum ii. F. Clements

  iii. **E. Heckel** iv. C. Ealton

- 'Ecosystem' the term was given by

  i. **A. C. Tansley** ii. E. Odum

  iii. E. Haeckel iv. C. Ealton

- The study of individual organism is called

  i. Synecology ii. **Autecology**

  iii. Hexicology iv. None of the above

- The sea anemone and hermit crab association is called

  i. **Symbiosis** ii. Mutualism

  iii. Commensalism iv. Parasitism

- Cold blooded animals are known as

  i. Steno therms ii. Cryophilic

  iii. **Poikilotherms** iv. Eurytherms

- In a lake, a condition Thermocline is

  i. **Rapid change in temperature**

  ii. Highest temperature

  iii. Lowest temperature

  iv. Constant temperature

- Best indicator for presence of pathogen in water is

  i. **Coliform bacteria** ii. Algae

  iii. Protozoa iv. Amoeba

- The law of minimum in ecology is proposed by

  i. **Liebig** ii. Odum

  iii. Tansley iv. Bergman

- The biggest mangrove forest in India is

  i. **Sunderban** ii. Andaman

  iii. Gulf of Kutch iv. Mannar strait

- In a pond the zone does not receive light is

  i. **Profundal zone** ii. Littoral zone

  iii. Limnetic zone iv. Necton zone

- Helophytes re

  i. **Marshy plants** ii. Desert plant

  iii. Aquatic plant iv. Terrestrial plant

- Psammophytes grows on

  i. Rocks and stone ii. **Sand and gravel**

  iii. Saline soils iv. Marshes

- Stomata are absent in

  i. Aquatic helophytes ii. **Submerged hydrophytes**

  iii. Emergent hydrophytes iv. Lithophytes

- Among the most efficient plant to trap light energy are sugarcane and corn because

  i. The have C3 acid cycle of photosynthesis

  ii. **They have C4 acid cycle of photosynthesis**

  iii. The possess photorespiration capability

  iv. They respond to fertilizers maximum

- Largest number of river valley projects present in

  i. USA ii. **India**

  iii. China iv. Russia

- Which of the following was found previously in India?

  i. **Cheetah** ii. Dodo

  iii. Panda iv. Leopard

- Endangered animals are listed in India in

  i. **Wildlife protection act, 1972**

  ii. Environment (protection) act, 1986

  iii. Forest conservation act, 1980

  iv. Indian forest act (revised), 1982

- Recommended forested area in hilly area is

  i. 40 % ii. 33 %

  iii. **60 %** iv. 50 %

- The first Indian biosphere reserve is

  i. Sunderbans ii. Nanda devi

  iii. **Nilgiri** iv. Kaziranga

- Symbiotic nitrogen fixation is found in

  i. **Rhizobium** ii. Usnea

  iii. Morcella iv. Blue green algae

- The microbe is harboured by root nodules of pulses

  i. Volvox ii. Anabaena

  iii. **Rhizobium** iv. Lactobacillus

- In Nitrification process

  i. **Ammonia is converted into nitrate**

  ii. Ammonia is converted into nitrite

  iii. Nitrate is converted into ammonia

  iv. Nitrate is converted into nitrite

- The biggest atmospheric hydrocarbon source in the atmosphere is

  i. **Petroleum burning** ii. Refuse burning

  iii. Coal burning iv. Power generation

- Pollutant emitted when in automobiles methanol is used as fuel

  i. NO_x ii. CO

  iii. **Formaldehyde** iv. PAN

- Carbamates are a group of

  i. **Pesticides**

  ii. Chemical enhancing biodegradation

  iii. Disinfectant chemical

  iv. O_3 friendly refrigerants

- Flame photometer can analyse

  i. **Sodium** ii. Chromium

  iii. Lead iv. Mercury

- In atmosphere the major anthropogenic source of sulphur dioxide is

  i. **Petrol** ii. Diesel

  iii. Coal iv. Wood

- Environmental estrogen, a pollutant that can mimic hormones is

  i. **Dioxins** ii. Vinyl chloride

  iii. Carbamates iv. Marcaptans

- Under section 49 of the Water (Preservation and control of pollution) Act, 1974, notice to a polluting industry is given for

  i. **60 days** ii. 30 days

  iii. 90 days iv. 10 days

- For handling food processing waste the best way is

  i. Burn the waste in incinerator

  ii. **Compost the waste in mixed form**

  iii. Treat it by aerobic treatment

  iv. Treat it by anaerobic treatment

- The material which can be recycled in easiest way and that can creates minimum pollution is

  i. Iron ii. **Glass**

  iii. Aluminium iv. Plastic

- The country that has world's best waste management and recycling programme?

  i. Germany ii. India

  iii. **Japan** iv. USA

- In biodegradable plastics which of the following chemical presents?

  i. Cross linked glycols ii. Straight glycols

  iii. **Poly hydroxyl butyrate** iv. Biodegradable cellulose

- The bioremediation technique is which of the following?

  i. **Composting** ii. Oxidation

  iii. Purging of air iv. Reduction

- To degrade complex substrate like lignin the white rot fungus is

  i. *Trichoderma chrysosporium* ii. ***Phanerochaete chrysosporium***

  iii. *Penicillium ressi* iv. *Chrysosporium ressi*

- In a paper and pulp industry the odour is mainly due to

  i. **Mercaptans** ii. Ammonia

  iii. Sulphaides iv. Dioxins

- Partially biodegradable plastics ar0e produced from

  i. **Corn starch and plastics**

  ii. Polyethylene and rubber

  iii. Polystyrene with saw dust

  iv. Cellulose and plastics

- In daily life the best and significant example of reuse is

  i. Sending old cars to recycling units

  ii. Recycling plastic carry bags

  iii. **Using glass bottles for beverage packing**

  iv. Recycling aluminium beverage cans

- To control accidental release of MIC, the safety devices installed in the Union carbide factory, Bhopal was

  i. GAC absorption and flaring

  ii. Flare

  iii. Scrubber

  iv. **Scrubber and flare**

- For implementation of ambient air quality standards which is not among sensitive area?

  i. Tourist resort ii. **Hospital**

  iii. National monuments iv. National parks

- Acute lead poisoning is

  i. Bysinnosis ii. Neuralgia

  iii. Itai-itai iv. **Plumbism**

- The tissue that is the best indicator of lead accumulation in human body is

  i. **Blood** ii. Fatty tissue

  iii. Bones iv. Brain

- Dams release the greenhouse gas is

  i. **CH_4** ii. CO

  iii. CO_2 iv. CFC

- Following of which is not a major soil pollution source?

  i. Coal based thermal power plant

  ii. **Coal mining**

  iii. Textile unita

  iv. Landfilling of municipal waste

- Which city receives highest cosmic radiation?

  i. **Delhi** ii. Bombay

  iii. Madras iv. Calcutta

- Black lung disease is found in

  i. Paint industry ii. **Coal mines**

  iii. Organic solvent industry iv. Electroplating industry

- pH of rainwater in unpolluted region is

  i. **5.6** ii. 6.5

  iii. 7.0 iv. 6.7

- The cleanest fuel is

  i. Gasoline ii. Coke

  iii. **Natural gas** iv. Diesel

- To generate energy the substance used in Magneto hydrodynamic generator is

  i. Tar sands ii. Oil shale

  iii. Uranium iv. **Coal**

- Which industry consumes largest coal in India?

  i. Cement industry ii. Steel industry

  iii. Fertilizer industry iv. **Thermal power plant**

- Chernobyl disaster was due to

  i. Failure in movement of control rods

  ii. Reaction of molten sodium with cooling water

  iii. **Reactor meltdown resulting from loss of cooling**

  iv. Entry of cooling water in reactor

- Geothermal energy extracted in

  i. Kangra valley, Himanchal

  ii. Kashmir valley

  iii. Sor valley, Pithoragarh

  iv. **Puga valley, Ladakh**

- Least damaging to environment is

  i. **Hydroelectricity** ii. Hydrogen energy

  iii. Electricity from coal iv. Nuclear power

- By volume main constituents of coal gas is

  i. Hydrogen ii. Methane

  iii. Carbon dioxide iv. **Carbon monoxide**

- Maximum electrical efficient is

  i. **Gas turbine** ii. Fluidized bed combustion

  iii. Steam turbine iv. Combined cycle gas turbine

- After installation the cheapest source of electricity is

  i. **Photovoltaic unit** ii. OTEC

  iii. Hydroelectricity iv. Geothermal well

- The source of energy in a fuel cell is

  i. Thermal energy ii. **Chemical energy**

  iii. Magnetic force iv. Electrical energy

- World's largest non-fuel mineral resource producer is

  i. **USA** ii. UK

  iii. China iv. India

- The term fluvial is related to

  i. **Rivers** ii. Beaches

  iii. Volcanoes iv. Mountains

- The ground water pollutant posing threat to public health in West Bengal is

  i. Selenium ii. **Arsenic**

  iii. Fluoride iv. Lead

- Menkes disease is related to

  i. Nickel deficiency ii. Boron deficiency

  iii. Zn deficiency iv. **Copper deficiency**

- Abundantly found mineral in rock is

  i. **Silicates** ii. Carbonates

  iii. Chlorides iv. Sulphates

- Nodule from deep ocean contains

  i. **Mn, Fe, Ni** ii. Na and K

  iii. Cu iv. Mg and Al

- Best aquifer will be

  i. **Gravel bed** ii. Sand bed

  iii. Clay bed iv. Laterite

- Zinc mainly is found in which state of India?

  i. **Rajasthan** ii. Bihar

  iii. Madhya Pradesh iv. Jharkhand

- In urban areas the principle components of photochemical smog are

  i. SPM & NO_2

  ii. CO & SPM

  iii. **Oxides of nitrogen, ozone and hydrocarbons**

  iv. NO_2& SO_2

- The earthworm used for composting is

  i. Eisenia foetida ii. Octochaetona serrate

  iii. **Both** iv. None of them

- The endangered bird species is

  i. **Great Indian Mustard** ii. Black duck

  iii. Hangul iv. Kashmir stag

- In a lake the layers formed due to thermal stratification are

  i. Epilimnion, Midlimnion and Hyperlimnion

  ii. Epilimnion, Oligolimnion and Hypolimnion

  iii. **Epilimnion, Thermocline and Hypolimnion**

  iv. Hypolimnion, Midlimnion and Epilimnion

- Public Liability Insurance Act was enacted in the year of

  i. 1995 ii. 1990

  iii. **1991** iv. 1974

- $REDD^+$ initiatives include

  i. Forest investment programme

  ii. Forest carbon partnership facility

  iii. **Both**

  iv. None

- Size range of atmospheric aerosols is

  i. 150 μm to 200 μm ii. 100 μm to 200 μm

  iii. 5 nm to 100 nm iv. **5 μm to 100 μm**

- The International year of biodiversity is

  i. 2008 ii. **2010**

  iii. 2006 iv. 1972

- The pyramid that is never inverted

  i. **Pyramid of energy** ii. Pyramid of number

  iii. Pyramid of biomass iv. None

- Most toxic state of Chromium is

  i. Cr^{+4} ii. Cr^{+3}

  iii. **Cr^{+6}** iv. Cr^{+2}

- After the environmental clearance, upto how many years the EIA report of a hydropower project would be valid?

  i. 30 years ii. 20 years

  iii. **10 years** iv. 5 years

- In which year Ramsar convention on wetland come into force?

  i. 1971 ii. **1975**

  iii. 1980 iv. 1985

- Laterite soil contains more of

  i. Magnesium and boron

  ii. **Iron and aluminium**

  iii. Aluminium and magnesium

  iv. Iron and boron

- Minimum stock height incinerators should be

  i. **30 m** ii. 25 m

  iii. 40 m iv. 10 m

- Removal of top fertile soil by water is termed as

  i. Siltation ii. Leaching

  iii. **Soil erosion** iv. Soil weathering

- The cause of pulmonary oedema is

  i. **Nitrous oxide** ii. Carbon monoxide

  iii. Sulphur dioxide iv. Methane

- Which is a type of in-situ conservation?

  i. Zoological park ii. Botanical park

  iii. Gene bank iv. **Wildlife sanctuaries**

- Pitch blende is

  i. Iron ore ii. Gold ore

  iii. **Uranium ore** iv. Lead ore

- Baba Amte lead

  i. Chipko movement

  ii. Appiko movement

  iii. **Narmada bachao andolon**

  iv. Tehri dam movement

- The pyramid of biomass was invented in

  i. Greenland ecosystem ii. Forest ecosystem

  iii. **Aquatic ecosystem** iv. Grassland ecosystem

- Largest source of freshwater is

  i. **Polar ice** ii. Rivers

  iii. Lake iv. Glaciers

- In normal rain water the acidity is due to

i. SO_2 ii. Cl_2

iii. NO_2 iv. **CO_2**

- The area where two major communities meet and blend together is called

i. Ecotype ii. **Ecotone**

iii. Ecosystem iv. Biotype

- A hazardous waste has character

i. Ignitibility ii. Reactivity

iii. Toxicity iv. **All of the above**

- Lightning in atmosphere produces

i. **NO** ii. NH_3

iii. CO iv. CO_2

- Phosphorous in living organisms largely associated with

i. Lipid ii. Protein

iii. Carbohydrate iv. **Nuclic acids**

- Net primary productivity of an ecosystem is

i. The primary productivity at consumer level

ii. The primary productivity at herbivore level

iii. The productivity at top consumer level minus respiration at all levels

iv. **The gross primary productivity minus plant respiration**

- Higher percentage of volatile matter present in which coal?

i. Bituminous ii. Anthracite

iii. Lignite iv. **Peat**

- For plant most important form of water is
  - i. **Capillary water**
  - ii. Hygroscopic water
  - iii. Gravitational water
  - iv. Combined water
- Mycorrhizae is an example of
  - i. Commensalism
  - ii. Ammensalism
  - iii. **Symbiosis**
  - iv. Parasitism
- Free living nitrogen fixer is
  - i. Rhizobium
  - ii. Frankia
  - iii. Dorylimes
  - iv. **Azotobactor**
- Azolla pinnata is
  - i. Red algae
  - ii. **Fern**
  - iii. Green algae
  - iv. Blue green algae
- Ecomark is
  - i. Label given to non-recyclable product
  - ii. **Label given to an environment friendly product**
  - iii. Label given to recycled product
  - iv. None of above
- The wavelength range of UV-C radiation is
  - i. 320-400 nm
  - ii. **200-280 nm**
  - iii. 180-240 nm
  - iv. 280-320 nm
- In a new area establishment of a species is called
  - i. Aggregation
  - ii. Migration
  - iii. **Ecesis**
  - iv. Stabilisation

- Among total dissolved matter in marine water, chlorine accounts for

  i. 12% ii. 24%

  iii. 30% iv. **55%**

- The term of Kyoto protocol has been extended beyond December 2012 by

  i. 10 years ii. **5 Years**

  iii. 15 years iv. 7 years

- The mineral that is most resistant to chemical weathering is

  i. **Quartz** ii. Feldspar

  iii. Olivine iv. Biotite

- For agriculture the good soil type is

  i. **Latosols** ii. Podozols

  ii. Serpent soil iv. Solonachak

- Peroxyacetyl Nitrate is formed by oxidation of

  i. Hydrocarbon ii. Terpene

  iii. Isoprene iv. **All of above**

5

Entomology & Nematology

Multiple Choice Based Questions and Answers

- Galea is a part of

  a) Mandibles b) Antennae

  c) **Maxillae** d) Leg

- Lacinia is a part of

  a) Mandibles b) Antennae

  c) **Maxillae** d) Leg

- Coxa is a part of

  a) **Leg** b) Antennae

  c) Mouth d) Wing

- Trochanter is a part of

  a) Mouth b) Wing

  c) **Leg** d) Antennae

- Femur is a part of

  a) Mouth b) Antennaee

  c) Wing d) **Leg**

- Galea is modified to from a coiled spring in which part of mouth part

  a) Sponging type b) Chewing lapping type

  c) **Siphoning type** d) Piercing and sucking type

- Prognathus type of head is found in
  - a) Grasshopper
  - b) Bug
  - c) **Beetles**
  - d) Termite

- Hypognathus type of head is found in
  - a) Bug
  - b) **Grasshopper**
  - c) Beetle
  - d) Butterfly

- The all individuals of class insecta are
  - a) 5 pairs of leg
  - b) 2 pairs of leg
  - c) **3 pairs of leg**
  - d) 4 pairs of leg

- The main important character of Arthropoda is
  - a) 3 pairs of leg
  - b) **Joint leg**
  - c) Shell over body
  - d) Unsegmented body

- The animals of Chilopod are
  - a) Herbivores
  - b) Polyphagous
  - c) **Insectivores**
  - d) Omnivores

- Crab belong to which class
  - a) Onychophora
  - b) Arachnida
  - c) **Crustacea**
  - d) Myriapoda

- The 4 pairs of legs are found in
  - a) Scorpion
  - b) **Mite**
  - c) Crab
  - d) Insect

- The five pairs of legs are found in
  - a) Scorpion
  - b) Mite
  - c) **Crab**
  - d) Insect

- Chelicerae are present in

a) Mite b) Crab

c) Insect d) **Scorpion**

- Antennae are absent in

a) Thysanura b) Collembolla

c) **Protura** d) Neuroptera

- First pairs of legs is modified into poison claw

a) Myriapoda b) Insecta

c) **Chilopoda** d) Arachnid

- The functions of malpignian tubules is

a) Digestion b) Respiration

c) **Excretion** d) Circulation

- The excretion in crustacians

a) Shell glands b) Green glands

c) **All of these** d) Coxal glands

- The respiration in crustacians by means of

a) Body surface b) Gills

c) Green glands d) **A+B**

- Johnston organ present in

a) Pedicel b) 2nd Segment of antennae

c) 3rd Segment of antennae d) **A+B**

- Taste organ are found in

a) Ants b) Honey bee

c) **Cockroach** d) Grasshopper

- Sound producing organs are located in the antennae of

a) Coleopterous | b) Orthopterous insect
c) Dipterous | d) **A+B**

- Hearing organs are found in

a) Male mosquito | b) Green butterfly
c) Paper wasp | d) **All of these**

- Serrate type of antennae found in

a) Grasshopper | b) Moth
c) Butterfly | d) **Pulsebeetle**

- Whorled type of antennae are found in

a) Panted bug | b) Water bug
c) Red cotton bug | d) **Male of mango mealy bug**

- Pectinate type of antennae are found in

a) Butterfly | b) Beetle
c) Honey bee | d) **Sugarcane root borrer**

- Plumose type of antennae are found in

a) Moth | b) Butterfly
c) **Male mosquito** | d) Female mosquito

- Moniliform type of antennae are found in

a) Termite | b) Thrips
c) **A+B** | d) Grass hopper

- Flagellum is the part of

a) Insect leg | b) Mouth
c) A+B | d) **Insect antennae**

- Fusiform type of antennae are found in

  a) Grasshopper b) Tobacco caterpillar

  c) Honey bee d) **Sphinged moth**

- Which type of mouth part are found in honey bee

  a) Sponging type b) Biting and cutting

  c) **Chewing lapping type** d) Sin phoning type

- Which type of mouth part are found in Thrips

  a) Sponging type b) Siphoning type

  c) **Rasping and sucking type** d) Chewing lapping type

- Piercing and sucking type of mouth part are found in

  a) Bug b) Mosquito

  c) Butterfly d) **A+B**

- Ambulatorial type of legs are found in

  a) Cockroach b) Bugs

  c) **A+B** d) Grasshopper

- Saltatorial or jumping type of antennae are found in

  a) Termite b) Mantis

  c) **Grasshopper** d) Bugs

- Fossorial or digging type of legs are found in

  a) Male cricket, nymphs of Gryllotulpa

  b) Cicada, Grubs of Scarabids and carabids

  c) Termites

  d) **Both A and B**

❒ Which type of legs are found in Mantis

a) Fossorial or digging type

b) Natatorial or swimming type

c) **Raptorial or Grasping type**

d) Jumping type

❒ Axillary region is located at the base of

a) The legs b) **The wings**

c) The antennae d) The mouth

❒ Father of biological classification is

a) J.C.Fabricius b) Pling

c) **Aristole** d) Carolus Linnaus

❒ The father of taxonomy is

a) Aristole b) **Carolus Linnaus**

c) J.C. Koening d) J.C.Fabricius

❒ Destructive insect pest Act enforced in

a) 1917 b) 1939

c) **1914** d) 1943

❒ Jugal and humeral lobe (coupling device) is commonly found in

a) Lepidoptera b) Trichoptera

c) Mecopterad. d) **All of these**

❒ Hamuli is found in

a) Lepidoptera b) Coleptera

c) **Hymenoptera** d) Orthropoda

- The amplexi form coupling apparatus is commonly met in the insects belonging to

  a) Papilionidae. b) bombycidae

  c) **A+B** d) Crysomelidae

- In grasshopper which type of wings are found

  a) Strepsipterab. b) **Tagmina**

  c) Dipterad. d) Elyetra

- Pseudo halters are found in which insect order

  a) Dipterab. b) Hymenoptera

  c) **Strepsiptera** d) Coleptera

- Rectum is a part of

  a) Foregut b) Midgut

  c) **Hind gut** d) Midgut and Hindgut

- Colon is a part of

  a) Fore gut b) Mid gut

  c) Hind gut d) Fore gut or mid gut

- Intima layer is in

  a) T. S. of crop b) T.S. of Gizzard

  c) **Both a and b** d) T.S. of mesenteron

- The regenerative cell are found in

  a) T.S. of Gizzard b) T.S. of crop

  c) Both a and b d) **T.S. of mesenteron**

- The main function of regenerative cell is

  a) **Renew and destroyed dead epithelial cells**

  b) To absorb the water

  c) To absorb the digested food

  d) To make digestive enzymes

- Stomodaeum is divided into
  - a) Phary, oesophagous
  - b) Crop, Gizzard
  - c) Both a and b
  - d) **Pyrynx, osophagous crop and gizzard**

- Trachea is originated from
  - a) Endoderm
  - b) **Ectoderm**
  - c) Both a and b
  - d) Mesoderm

- All spiracles are open in
  - a) Larva of mosquito
  - b) Pupa of mosquito
  - c) **Grasshopper**
  - d) Maggot of housefly

- The anterior most pair of spiracles is functional and remaining are closed in
  - a) **Mosquito pupa**
  - b) Mosquito larva
  - c) Maggot of housefly
  - d) Grubs

- The first and last pair of spiracles are functional in
  - a) **Maggot of** housefly
  - b) Larva of mosquito
  - c) Pupa of mosquito
  - d) Grasshopper

- Photoreceptor or visual organs are
  - a) Dermal light sense
  - b) Ocellus or simple eyes
  - c) Compound eyes
  - d) **All of these**

- Chordotonal or scolopophorous organs are
  - a) Tympanal organ
  - b) Johnston's organ
  - c) **Both a and b**
  - d) Leg

❒ Silver fish belongs to the order

a) **Thysanura** b) Diplura

c) Protura d) Collembola

❒ Japygids are found in

a) **Diplura** b) Diptera

c) Trichoptera d) Mechoptera

❒ Spring tails are found in the order

a) Siphunculata b) Zoraptera

c) **Collembola** d) Mallophaga

❒ Mayfly comes under the order

a) Odonata b) Phasmida

c) Dermeptera d) **Ephemeroptera**

❒ Stonefly comes under the order

a) Psocoptera b) Dermeptera

c) **Plecoptera** d) Thysanoptera

❒ Book lice comes under the order

a) **Psocoptera** b) Mallophaga

c) Sipnunculata d) Embioptera

❒ Sucking lice are found under the order

a) Mallophaga b) **Siphunculata**

c) Psocoptera d) Embioptera

❒ Scorpion fly comes under the order

a) Neuroptera b) Trichoptera

c) **Mecoptera** d) Strepsiptera

- Caddis fly comes under the order

  a) Mecoptera b) **Trichoptera**

  c) Strepsiptera d) Neuroptera

- Larva of housefly is called as

  a) Grub b) **Maggot**

  c) Nymph d) Caterpillar

- Larva of butterfly is known as

  a) Grub b) Maggot

  c) Nymph d) **Caterpillar**

- Larva of beetle is known as

  a) Caterpillar b) Nymph

  c) **Grub** d) Maggot

- The immature stage of grasshopper is called as

  a) Larva b) Maggot

  c) **Nymph** d) Caterpillar

- Scarabacid form larva are found in which order

  a) **Coleoptera** b) Lepidoptera

  c) Diptera d) Hemiptera

- Exarate adecticous pupa are found in

  a) Hymenoptera b) Diptera

  c) Lepidoptera d) **Coleoptera**

- Locust warning organization was established in which year...............

  a) 1938

  b) 1914

  c) 1939

  d) 1997

- National Center for Integrated Pest Management located at.............

  a) Kanpur b) kerla

  c) Banglore d) New Delhi

- Digestive system of insect from mouth to anus called..........................

  a) Midgut b) Hindgut

  c) Foregut d) Alimentary Canal

- Honey chamber is a part of alimentary canal in which worker bees store nectar in modified form of ....

  a) Gizzard b) Crop

  c) Intima d) Epithellium

- In termite cellulose is digested by............

  a) Bacteria b) Virus

  c) Nematode d) Protozoa

- Which insecticides is used for seed dressing ....

  a) Malathion b) Endosulfan

  c) A+B d) Imidaclopride

- Haemocytes are derived from embryonic......

  a) Endoderm b) Mesoderm

  c) A+B d) Mesoderm

- Yellow mosaic virus is transmitted by..........

  a) Aphid b) Jassids

  c) A+B d) Whitefly

- Moulting hormone (Ecdysone) aresecreted from which gland?

  a) Corpora cardiac b) Corpora allatata

  c) A+B d) Prothoracic gland

- Stemmata is found in..............

  a) Nymph b) Adult

  c) A+B d) Larva

- The Lace wings (*Chrysoperla carnea)* is predator of ....

  a) Larva b) Pupa

  c) Adult d) Aphids

- The true fly is known as..............

  a) White fly b) House fly

  c) A+B d) House fly

- Fruit dropping in mango s due to attack of.........

  a) Red cotton bug b) Mango stem borrer

  c) A+B d) Mango mealy Bug

- The sulfur is used against which ....

  a)Aphid b) Borer

  c) Beetle d) Mite

- Polyphagous pest is ....

  a) Aphid b) Mango mealy bug

  c) White grub d) Chillopartelus

- Locust & Female Grasshopper lay eggs in................

  a) Upper side of leaves b) Lower side of leaves

  c) In side stem d) In the soil

- The dead heart in Jowar is caused by...................

  a) Chillopartelus b) Grasshopper

  c) Root borer d) Pink boll worm

- The larva look like bird excreta..................

  a) Larva of cabbage butterfly b) Larva of monarch butterfly

  c) Larva of lemon butterfly d) Larva of swallow tail butterfly

- Red pumpkin beetle lay eggs in............

  a) Stem b) Soil

  c) Lower side of leaves d) Upper side of leaves

- Achoea janata is the pest of

  a) Castor b) Mango

  c) Potato d) Apple

- *Coccinella*is an effective predator of.........

  a) Beetle b) Aphid

  c) Butterfly d) Grasshopper

- Early sowing of mustard escapes the infestation of........

  a) Aphid b) Painted bug

  c) Saw fly d) Helicoverpa

- Polyphagous insect is.....

  a) Locust b) Helicoverpa

  c) Aphid **d) A+B**

- Rice Gandhi bug lays eggs on..............

  a) Upper side of leaves b) Lower side of leaves

  c) Rice Ear d) Soil

- Which of the following insect is not considerd in bollworm group of cotton

  a) Helicoverpa b) Spotted boll worm

  c) Pink Boll worm **d) Leaf Roller**

- Which insect is responsible for bunchy top disease

  a) Chilo incertulas b) Amsacta albistiga

  c) Pyrilla **d) Scirpophaga nivella**

- African marigold is considered as trap crop for…

  a) Gram Pod Borer b) Tomato Fruit Borer

  c) A+B d) Pink boll worm

- Mango melay bug lay egg on……..

  a) Stem b) Inflorescence

  c) Soil d) Leaf

- *Eublemma- amabilis* is predator of

  a) Silk moth b) Lac insect

  c) Aphid d) Honey

- *Galleria mellonella* feeds on

  a) Honey b) Bee wax

  c) Silk d) A+B

- The tassar silk worm feeds………..

  a) Mulberry Leaves **b) Castor Leaves**

  c) Potato leaves d) All of these

- Royal jelly is secreted by……….

  a) Queen b) **Worker Bee**

  c) Drone d) All of these

- 90% of lac is obtained from………..

  a) Kusumi **b) Rangeeni**

  c) A+B d) None of these

- The maximum ilk is produced in

  a) Karnataka b) Tamil Nadu

  c) Kerala d) A.P

- *Apis dorsata* is commonly known as

  a) Rock Bee b) Indian bee

  c) Little Bee d) Dammar Bee

- *Apis indica*is commonly known as

  a) Rock Bee **b) Indian Bee**

  c) Little Bee d) Dammar Bee

- *Apis florea* is commonly known as

  a) Indian Bee b) Rock Bee

  c) Little Bee d) Dammar Bee

- *Milipona* is commonly known as

  a) Dammar Bee b) Indian Bee

  c) Rock Bee d) Little Bea

- *Apis mellifera* is commonly known as

  a) Indian Bee b) Rock Bee

  c) European Bee d) None of these

- Nosema disease is caused by

  a) Viral **b) Protozoa**

  c) Mite d) Amoeba

- Acarine disease is caused by

  a) Mite b) Virus

  c) Bacteria d) Protozoa

- Tassar silk worm is commonly known as

  a) Antherae paphia b) Antherae assamia

  c) Philosamia ricini d) Thipaila religiosae

- Eri silk worm is commonly known as

  a) Philosamia ricini b) Antherae paphia

  c) Antherae assamia d) Thiopaila religiosae

- Munga silk worm is commonly known as

  a) ***Antherae assamia*** b) *Antherae paphia*

  c) *Philosamia ricini* d) *Thiopaila religiosae*

- Deo muga silk worm is commonly known as

  a) ***Thiopaila religiosae*** b) *Antherae paphia*

  c) *Antherae assamia* d) *Philosamia ricini*

- Pebrine disease is

  a) Viral b) Protozoan

  c) A+B d) None of these

- Grasserie disease is caused by...

  a) Bacteria b) Viral

  c) Protozoa d) Fungi

- Flacherie disease of silk worm is caused by…

  a) Bacteria **b) Indigestion**

  c) Fungi d) None of these

- *Rodolia-cardinalis*is predator of

  a) Cottony cushion scale b) Aphelinus mali

  c) Bracon gelechae d) Sanjose scale

- *Aphelinus mali*is parasite of..........

  a) Wooly Aphid b) Potato tuber moth

  c) Sanjose scale d) Jowar stem borer

- *Prospaltella perniciosi* is parasite of.........

  a) Sanjose scale b) Coconut caterpillar

  c) Grasshopper d) Jowar stem borer

- *Spoggosia beniziana* is parasite of

  a) Coconut caterpillar b) Jowar stem borer

  c) Caster semilooper d) Hairy caterpillar

- *Telonomus nawai* is parasite of..............

  a) Castor semilooper b) Jowar stem borer

  c) Coconut caterpillar d) Sanjose scale

- Systematic insecticides are ....

  a) Contact poison **b) Stomach poison**

  c) A+B d) None of these

- The insecticidal properties of D.D.T was discovered by.....

  a) M. Faraday **b) Paul Muller**

  c) Butler d) None of them

- The concept of I.P.M was first proposed by.......

  a) Geier b) Clark

  c) None of these d) A+B

- *Hellula undalis* disease is caused by...

  a) Cabbage Borer b) Diamond black moth

  c) Cabbage Fly d) Cabbage Butterfly

- *Plulella sp.* Is commonly known as

  a) Diamond Black Moth b) Aphid

  c) Cabbage Borer d) Cabbage Butterfly

- *Phytomyza articonnis* disease is caused by.........

  a) Leaf miner b) Aphid

  c) Bug d) None of these

- *Euzophera perticella* disease is caused by..

  a) Brinjal stem borer b) Tomato fruit borer

  c) Cabbage borer d) None of these

- Indian Institute of National Gums & Resins is located ....

  a) Ranchi b) Kolkata

  c) Bengaluru d) Lucknaw

- National Centre for Integrated Pest Management is located .....

  a) Bengaluru b) Kolkata

  c) New Delhi d) Karnal

- National Bureau of Agriculture Insect Resources is located at

  a) Bengaluru b) New Delhi

  c) Hyderabad d) Karnal

- The whole upper region of insect head is form...

  a) Epicranium b) Clypeus

  c) Labrum d) Gena

- The entire lateral region of head capsule below & behind the compound eyes is known as....

  a) Epicarnium b) Clypeus

  c) Labrum d) Gena